Caldecott Connections to Social Studies

Caldecott Connections to Social Studies

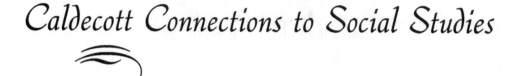

Shan Glandon

2000
Libraries Unlimited
A Division of Greenwood Publishing Group, Inc.
Englewood, Colorado

*To students as they work as historians and geographers,
exploring their heritages and the cultures of the world.*

Libraries Unlimited
A Division of Greenwood Publishing Group, Inc.
P.O. Box 6633
Englewood, CO 80155-6633
1-800-237-6124
www.lu.com

Library of Congress Cataloging-in-Publication Data

Glandon, Shan.
    Caldecott connections to social studies / Shan Glandon.
       p. cm.
    Includes bibliographical references (p.) and index.
    ISBN 1-56308-845-2 (pbk.)
       1. Social studies--Study and teaching (Elementary)--United States--Curricula. 2. Caldecott Medal. 3. Illustrated children's books--Study and teaching--United States. 4. Education, Elementary--Activity programs--United States. I. Title.

LB1584 .G48 2000
372.83'044--dc21   00-030249

Contents

Figures and Activity Sheets

Figures

Activity Sheets

Introduction

➤ Connecting to the Curriculum

Caldecott Award literature provides rich fuel for teaching, extending, and enriching curriculum objectives. The award winners are engaging stories that offer vivid vocabulary images, use art in varied ways, and spark links to each of the major curriculum areas.

Students may begin the year with a look at Randolph Caldecott and the award itself (see the lesson on introducing Randolph Caldecott and reading the honor books on page 149), and Caldecott Award posters may be displayed in the classroom and the library as a constant visual reminder of all the stories that have won. (Caldecott Award posters are available from Perma-Bound, 617 East Vandalia Rd., Jacksonville, IL 62650, 1-800-637-6581, cost, $2.00.) The Caldecott Medal, named in honor of Randolph Caldecott, a nineteenth-century children's book illustrator, has been awarded annually since 1938 to an American illustrator for the most distinguished picture book published during the previous year. When reviewing books for the award, committee members look for excellence in artistic technique as well as in integrating the text of the story into the pictorial interpretation. Randolph Caldecott was chosen because he established new directions in illustrating children's books. His illustrations were drawn with the child in mind; they have humor and imagination and are filled with lifelike characters, lots of action, and many details. The Caldecott Web site (http://www.ala.org/alsc/ caldecott.html) can be bookmarked and students can browse it for further information and enjoyment.

➤ Connecting to Art

Connections with art teachers are a natural result of a focus on Caldecott Award literature and offer opportunities for students to try different illustrating techniques as they explore line, color, tone, and balance in art. After reading *Grandfather's Journey*, students can create their own imaginative watercolor scenes of favorite memories from childhood. They can make wonderful animal masks to dramatize *May I Bring a Friend?* by using large brown paper bags, black markers for outlining and details, and tempera paints for filling in lines with bright colors. Investigating the effects of different kinds of lines (straight, curvy, thick, thin, and slanted) and geometric shapes assists students in creating petroglyph scenes and in imitating the art of *Arrow to the Sun*. While creating landscape pictures based on *The Girl Who Loved Wild Horses*, students can discover the effectiveness of placing real objects and found materials in their scenes. Watercolor paintings (like those in *The Little House*, *Hey, Al*, and *Officer Buckle and Gloria*) provide students with opportunities to play with color to express mood and feelings in art, while viewing the works of Diego Rivera (Mexican muralist) and colored pencil sketches give students ideas for creating the jungle mural of Mexico (*Nine Days to Christmas*). The Conté chalks allow students to explore light and shadow as they create pictures inspired by reading *Jumanji*.

Another method for helping students experience the variety of media used in illustrating Caldecott Award literature is to gather samples of the different media. Take a trip to an art supply store and purchase the following supplies: paint samples (oil, acrylic, watercolor, gouache, gesso, and tempera), paintbrushes, a pen with a number of nibs, inks (India and one other), pastels (oil and Conté), and colored pencils. As the stories are shared and the art techniques are discussed, show the appropriate media and demonstrate their uses.

➤ Connecting to Curriculum Units

Caldecott Award stories can become the springboard for introducing units of studies. The social studies explorations enhance global awareness and historical perspective and develop productive citizens; *Jumanji* explores biomes of the world; *Hey, Al* introduces the five themes of geography; *Arrow to the Sun*, *May I Bring a Friend?*, *Nine Days to Christmas*, and *The Little House* expand knowledge of the themes through further studies of desert regions, countries of the world, traditions and customs of Mexico, and students' local communities. Historical perspective increases as students look at Native American groups (*The Girl Who Loved Wild Horses*), pioneer life in America (*Ox-Cart Man*), their own family heritage (*Grandfather's Journey*), and biographies of world figures (*The Glorious Flight*). In the *Officer Buckle and Gloria* unit, students experience the value of teamwork and collaboration.

➤ Collaboration

Collaborations between classroom teachers and library media specialists facilitate implementation of the activities described in this book. The stories can be shared in the classroom or the library, and both the teacher and the librarian can assign, develop, and assess activities. The countries of the world unit (*May I Bring a Friend?*) requires this close connection because students have to make lengthy research investigations and have frequent opportunities to share products with many audiences. (The open space of the media center can make these presentations more effective.) In the Native American culture areas unit, which follows *The Girl Who Loved Wild Horses*, the library media specialist and the teacher can divide mentoring responsibilities and help student groups create products that show the lifestyles and customs of each culture area; students also use the library to select myths and legends for independent reading. Research is also a significant component of the Mexico unit (*Nine Days to Christmas*) as students find out about the country's geography and famous historical cities of Mexico. The library media specialist can be instrumental in providing the multiple resources needed for the communities unit based on *The Little House* and in helping students select biographies for independent reading as they develop awareness of people in history who have made a difference and construct a historical timeline (*The Glorious Flight*). Discovery centers offer independent exploration experiences and more in-depth studies, and the library can be a vital link in making these happen; several of the stories provide these learning opportunities (*Arrow to the Sun*, *The Ox-Cart Man*, and *The Girl Who Loved Wild Horses*). The space and resources of the library are more conducive to doing biome research and offer a large area in which to play the game of Jumanji, as well as provide research time for studying the history of communication (*Where the Wild Things Are*).

When implementing the *Jumanji* lesson plans, the following pattern of collaboration between the classroom and the library occurred: The story was introduced by the librarian; at the "Connect" stage of the lesson plan, the teacher showed the discovery center task cards and introduced the activities. Then the students returned to the classroom. (This particular teacher used centers as a way of organizing the class during his two literature circle times; while he worked with one small group, the rest of the students rotated through the centers.) During literature circle/center time, five activities took place: the literature circle meeting with the teacher and the discovery centers (set up in the classroom). While the teacher met with the first literature circle (usually for an hour), the rest of the students were divided among the discovery center activities. The students in the "reading" discovery center returned to the library in search of other stories by Van Allsburg. Sometimes they remained in the library to read the story and prepare and rehearse their book reviews; sometimes they returned to the classroom after checking out the book. This pattern of work was repeated while the teacher met with the second literature circle. The biome research project was introduced and completed in the library, and the entire class of students (with their teacher) came every day for a week for an hour of research. During the later stages of biome research, when students were actually constructing their game boards, the librarian and the teacher divided their efforts, with some students working in the library and some students working in the classroom. At the close of biome research, the student-made game boards were displayed on library tables; students presented their boards and then played the games. (Biome research was assessed by the librarian and recorded as a social studies grade in the classroom.) For the culminating game of Jumanji, the students prepared game cards in the classroom under the direction of the teacher, then came to the library to actually play the game.

The lessons resulting from sharing *Ox-Cart Man* followed this pattern of collaboration: The story was introduced in the library, and in the classroom the teacher followed the story with the Seasons of the Farm lesson plan and art project. (Students created a timeline showing a year of work and fun in farm life.) Although the Then and Now lesson plan took place in the classroom, during the "Explore" portion of the lesson, several student partnerships made trips to the library to consult sources on pioneer life to add to their comparison charts. The lesson plan, Experiencing the Life of a Pioneer, occurred in the library, and the discovery centers were placed around the library. Parent volunteers helped in each center, freeing the teacher and the librarian to circulate, observe, make anecdotal notes on students, and help where needed. The reflection discussion at the close of the discovery center experiences was jointly led by the teacher and the librarian and focused on making generalizations about pioneer life.

The library truly becomes an extension of the classroom and provides key ingredients for successful implementation of the lesson plans.

➤ Integrating Multiple Intelligences Theory and Practices

In *Frames of Mind: The Theory of Multiple Intelligences* (New York: Basic Books, 1983), Howard Gardner challenges the narrowly held definition of intelligence (based on an IQ score) and the context in which IQ had been measured (completing isolated tasks outside of a natural learning environment) and proposes a theory of multiple intelligences that identifies at least eight basic intelligences and defines intelligence as the capacity for solving problems and fashioning products in a context-rich and naturalistic setting. *Verbal/linguistic intelligence* is the capacity to use words effectively, either in writing (exemplified by poets, authors, playwrights, journalists, and editors) or in speaking (storytelling and debating). Students who evidence this intelligence pore over words, are fascinated with language, and use language effectively in speaking and/or writing. Those with *musical/rhythmic intelligence* respond to sounds and rhythms and enjoy and seek out opportunities to hear music, to improvise and play with sounds and rhythms, and to mentor with musicians. Notice these students: They often tap their feet or pencils, sometimes hum while working intently, and perk up when music or rhythm is used during a lesson. *Visual/spatial intelligence* is defined by an ability to see the visual/ spatial world accurately and to act upon those images through painting, drawing, designing, and sculpting. Because they see internally, students with highly developed visual/spatial intelligence are also often good at chess and navigation (finding their way in uncharted spaces); they may also be day-dreamers. These are the artists who love anything visual, who see images and pictures and draw their ideas. *Bodily/kinesthetic intelligence* is found in dancers, athletes, and inventors because of their prowess in using body movement to express ideas and feelings and to implement game plays or use their hands to create new products or transform things. Think of students who learn best by doing; if they can manipulate it, do it, create movements to learn it, then they develop understanding. *Logical/mathematical intelligence* involves skill with numbers and number manipulation and skill in strategies for reasoning— scientific, deductive, and inductive. Problem solving interests these students and they love the challenge of organizing and using numbers and developing charts, timelines, and graphs as expressions of thinking. Students with highly developed *interpersonal intelligence* easily communicate and work collaboratively with others; they are sensitive to feelings and moods. These students are good listeners who work well in collaborative situations and seem to get along with anyone. They have a knack for bringing out the best in each learner. *Intrapersonal intelligence* focuses on self-knowledge and the ability to act on the basis of that knowledge. These students are reflective, thoughtful learners who need to see the big picture and have time to fit new knowledge into current thinking; they enjoy building awareness of their own processes for learning. The eighth intelligence, *naturalist intelligence,* focuses on a student's ability to observe and make connections in living things (plants and animals) and in natural phenomena (clouds, rocks). This intelligence highlights the accomplishments of scientists in creating classification systems.

Gardner suggests that everyone possesses all eight intelligences, but some are highly developed, others more modestly developed, and still others relatively undeveloped, and that most people can develop each intelligence to an adequate level of competency. This understanding has implications for the organization and development of daily lesson plans because integration of multiple intelligences theory and practice expands opportunities for students to mobilize their full range of intellectual abilities and become thoroughly engaged in learning.

➤ Designing the Lessons

Best-practice principles emerging from state-of-the-art teaching in each curriculum field focus on learning that is student-centered (builds on students' natural curiosity), experiential (hands-on and active), holistic (involves big-picture ideas), authentic (involves encounters with complex and real ideas), expressive (demands the whole range of intelligence, art, music, writing, speaking, etc.), reflective (allows time to generalize and make connections), social (includes support of peers and mentors), collaborative (encourages working together rather than in competition), democratic (models the principles of living and working in a democracy), cognitive (demands higher-order thinking), developmental (involves learning experiences guided by the needs of the students), constructivist (builds, creates, and develops knowledge systems), and challenging (provides choices and responsibility for learning). Two books to read for more information about these principles are *Best Practice* by Steven Zemelman, Harvey Daniels, and Arthur Hyde (Heinemann, 1998), and *ITI: The Model, Integrated Thematic Instruction* by Susan Kovalik (Books for Educators, 1994). They can be ordered from Heinemann, 361 Hanover St., Portsmouth, NH 03801-3912, cost, $23.50, and Books for Educators, 17051 S. E. 272nd St., Suite 18, Kent, WA, 98042, cost, $27.50.

The "Engage, Elaborate, Explore, Connect" lesson plan format that I developed in 1994 is the organizing structure for the story units in this book. This lesson planning format integrates best-practice principles, builds a discovery approach to learning, promotes integration of multiple intelligences theory and practice, and lets teachers see, at a glance, diversity and flexibility in teaching.

Engage

Teachers use this one-to-three-minute step to engage the attention of the student; it's a wake up call to the brain—a way to start the brain thinking about patterns and relationships. Through a puzzling picture, a catchy musical piece, a challenging question, complicated body movements, a paradox, or a series of quick visual images, the "Engage" step provides the spark that captures the total interest of the students and prepares them for the lesson content. Some "Engage" sections include "quick think" activities. The goal of a quick think is to awaken the brain and have students begin to think in open-ended ways.

Elaborate

In this portion of the lesson, teachers use multiple intelligence strategies to elaborate important concepts and skills. Teachers may use stories, video footage, creative dramatics, debate, dance and movement, questioning, and rhythms to teach lesson content.

Explore

This step gives the students opportunities to explore lesson content and develop in-depth investigations and studies.

Connect

This is the step in which students make connections to real-world settings through reflection, generalization, synthesis, and transformation, thus enhancing the capacity for solving problems and fashioning products.

When using this organizing format, there are many starting points. Sometimes the "Explore" activity is clear in my mind and I work from that activity. I then decide what direct instruction is needed for successful completion of the activity. (This direct instruction becomes the "Elaborate" stage of the lesson.) With these two components developed, I think about capturing students' attention, awakening the brain for learning, and sparking an interest. The "Engage" step of the lesson helps students tune-in and get ready for the complexity of thought and work required for the rest of the lesson. Music, art, and movement are particularly effective attention-getters in the "Engage" step, and I enjoy challenging myself to use them. Then, based on these three components of the lesson, I think about making connections and demonstrating understandings and ask myself: How will students reflect on the activity and demonstrate and share what they have learned?

For social studies lessons, the "Explore" activity is often my starting point, and I imagine and think of activities that will allow students to work as historians, geographers, and social scientists in hands-on experiences and investigations, giving them frequent opportunities to reflect and make generalizations to build personal connections to social studies topics.

Caldecott Connections to Social Studies brings award-winning literature to the social studies curriculum. I hope you enjoy the fun and diversity offered in the activities and the noise and excitement produced when students are actively engaged in constructing knowledge. I also hope these activities inspire continuing connections for you and your students.

1 *Arrow to the Sun*

Adapted by Gerald McDermott
Illustrated by Gerald McDermott
New York: The Viking Press, 1974 (Filmstrip version: Weston Woods, 1975)

Summary

➤ Long ago the lord of the sun sent the spark of life to Earth and in this way the boy came into the world of men. When the boys of the pueblo mocked him because he had no father, the boy set out on a quest to find his father, traveling to the sun and proving himself in the four chambers of ceremony. He returned to Earth, empowered with the knowledge of his father.

Award Year

➤ 1975

Art Information

➤ Illustrated using gouache and ink.

Curriculum Connections

➤ Deserts

➤ Activity Plan 1: Sharing the Story

Materials

Map of deserts of the United States (figure 1.1)
Crayons
Large plate or tray (large enough to hold selected crayons)
Caldecott Award poster
Thin black permanent ink marker
Gouache paint (available at art stores)

Engage

As students gather for story time, have them select crayons that represent desert colors. Show a map of the major deserts in the United States and identify them. Discuss characteristics of deserts. Ask the students what colors they think represent desert colors. Have them stand and share choices as categories of colors are named. Make a color wheel on the large plate or tray with the crayons. (*Visual/Spatial Intelligence*)

Elaborate

Introduce *Arrow to the Sun*. This is a Pueblo Indian story; the Pueblo Indians lived in these desert areas of Arizona (look again at the map). Pose these questions for students to answer after listening and watching: How does the boy change? What does he learn about himself?

Explore

Read or show the story.

Connect

Ask the students these questions: Why did the sun test the boy? What did the four tests (lions, serpents, bees, lightning) prove to the boy? What does he learn about himself? How does the boy change? What do you think is the most important thing to remember from this story? If you were the boy, how would you have solved the problem?
Share the Caldecott Award information:

1. As students examine the cover of the book, ask them what special thing they notice. (gold medal) Ask them what the name of the medal is. (Caldecott Award Medal) Ask them why it has been placed on this book? (Some of the answers may be that the illustrations are special, well done, particularly interesting, exciting, and/or unusual.)

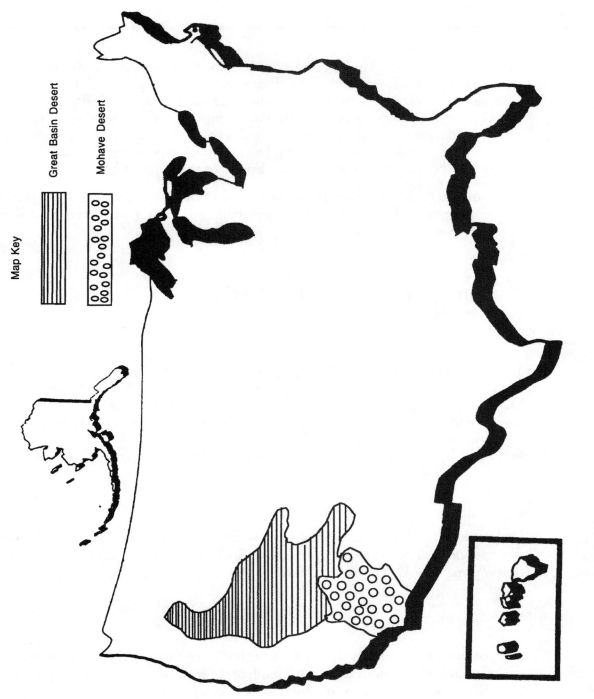

Map Key

Great Basin Desert

Mohave Desert

▶ Figure 1.1. Deserts of the United States

2. Discuss the art techniques used in creating the pictures. Ask students what adjectives they would use to describe these illustrations. (bright, bold, fiery, angular, sharp, geometric, active) In many of the pages the designs extend off the page, reinforcing the continuing action of the story. (Point out the tri-colored lines that begin after the page when the boy comes into the world of men. These lines continue on the pages that follow as the boy begins his journey in search of his father.) Gouache, a form of watercolor, has been used to create the bold colors.

3. Ask two student volunteers to search the poster for the year the story won. (Searching the poster helps students become familiar with the different titles selected for the award.)

➤ Activity Plan 2: What Causes a Desert?

Materials

Map of world deserts; make a transparency or enlarge it (see figure 1.2)
Masking tape
Marbles or some objects that can be dropped from students' hands
Two long sheets of butcher paper, measuring twenty-four inches by sixty inches (one in blue and one in brown)
Five signs: North, South, East, West, Mountain Barrier (see figure 1.3)

Engage

Look at the map of the world and identify the major deserts. Ask students to speculate about what has caused these deserts to form. (Answers may include: "not much rainfall" and "lots of sunshine.") (*Visual/Spatial and Verbal/Linguistic Intelligences*)

Elaborate

Use masking tape to mark three lines on the floor: the equator, the Tropic of Cancer (north of the equator), and the Tropic of Capricorn (south of the equator). Leave a space a yard wide between each line (see figure 1.4). Group four piles of marbles along the equator, about two feet apart. Invite two students to pretend to be the air and have them crouch at the equator near the marble piles. (The marbles represent moist and warm air and eventually rain.) They should be able to pick up the marbles in each hand. (*Bodily/Kinesthetic Intelligence*)

Text continues on page 7.

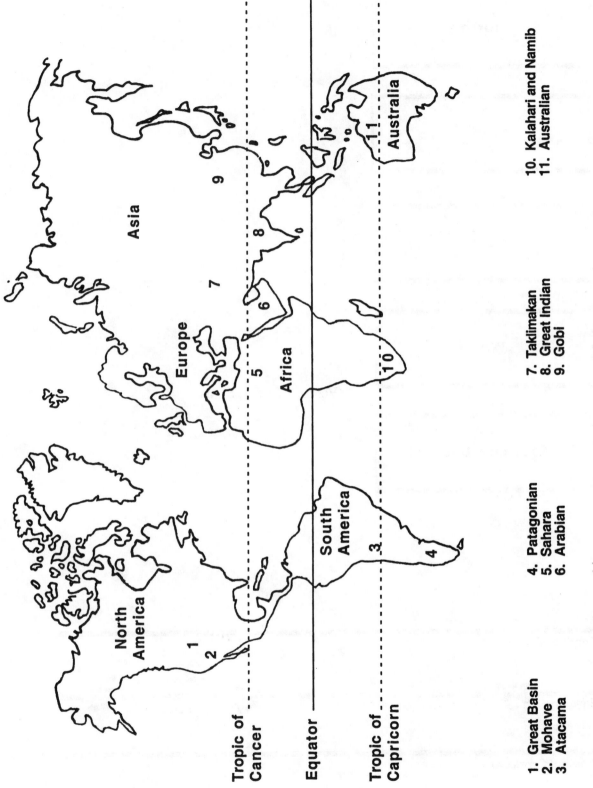

▶ Figure 1.2. Deserts of the World

1. Great Basin
2. Mohave
3. Atacama

4. Patagonian
5. Sahara
6. Arabian

7. Taklimakan
8. Great Indian
9. Gobi

10. Kalahari and Namib
11. Australian

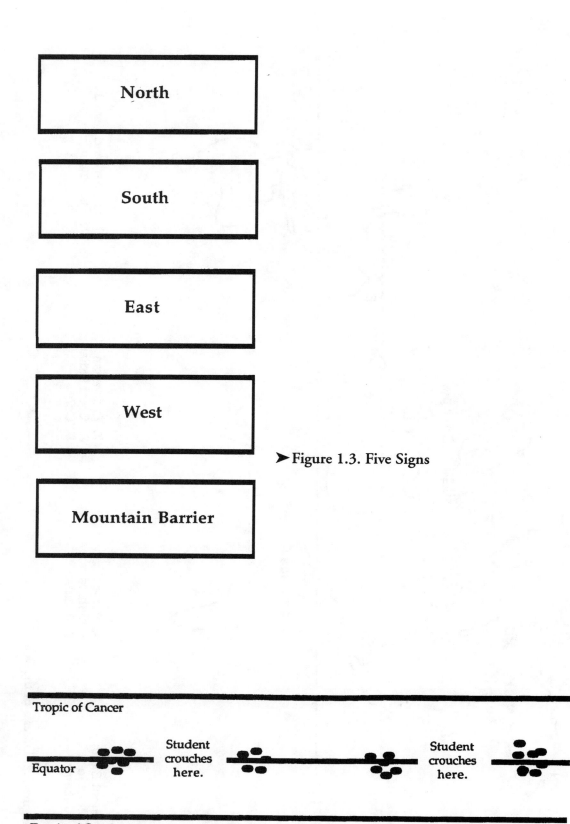

North

South

East

West

► Figure 1.3. Five Signs

Mountain Barrier

Tropic of Cancer

Student crouches here.

Student crouches here.

Equator

Tropic of Capricorn

► Figure 1.4. Prevailing Winds Demonstration

Provide the following narration while the students demonstrate what is happening:

Most deserts are formed north and south of the equator in two narrow areas that circle the Earth. The air around the equator is moist and warm and as it rises [have students pick up marble piles and slowly move to a standing position, with arms extended] and travels north or south, it drops its moisture and becomes drier and heavier. [Have students release the marbles. They should open their hands and let the marbles go, but not throw them. One student steps north two steps and one student steps south two steps. Their arms are at their sides after the marbles are released.] As these prevailing winds move north toward the Tropic of Cancer and south toward the Tropic of Capricorn, the heavier air descends. [Have students move north and south toward the tropic lines, and as they reach the tropic lines, swoop down, rotate in a circle, and blow hot air.] This air is very dry and this is where many deserts form.

Repeat this demonstration and ask other students to narrate and act.

Explore

The blockage of mountains is another way deserts form. This is called "the rain shadow" effect. Set up the following demonstration. Position the long strip of blue paper that represents the ocean; position the brown paper, representing land, next to it; place two chairs or stools to the right of the brown paper, then create a barrier next to the chairs or stools. Add the five signs (see figure 1.5). (*Bodily/Kinesthetic Intelligence*)

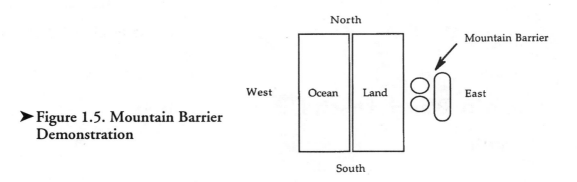

➤ **Figure 1.5. Mountain Barrier Demonstration**

Provide the following narration while the students demonstrate what is happening:

Winds sweep eastward across the ocean and bring moisture inland. [Have two students stand west of the ocean, holding the marbles, and as the narration begins, sweep across the blue strip and the brown strip and climb the chairs, facing the east.] As the moist air travels inland and meets a mountain barrier, it is forced to rise. It begins to cool down as it rises, clouds form, and rain falls on the westward slope of the mountain. [Have students extend their arms behind them and release the marbles.] The air that comes down on the eastward side of the mountain is drier and warmer. [Have students lean forward and blow hot air over the mountain barrier.] Very little rain falls here and deserts often form.

Repeat this demonstration and ask other students to narrate and act.

Return to the map of deserts of the world (see figure 1.2) and explain the third reason deserts form:

Deserts can also form along a coast because of the cold ocean currents flowing next to the continent. The Atacama Desert in South America and the Namib Desert in southwest Africa are examples of this effect. The cooling is caused by the Humboldt or Peru current off western South America and the Benguela current off southwest Africa. The cool winds that blow across the cold ocean currents carry very little moisture. As the winds move inland, the air becomes warmer and drier, thus creating desert conditions.

Connect

Have students work with partners to choose a desert of the world and research the desert's formation, using maps, globes, and maybe an encyclopedia. Create a chart listing how the deserts have formed (see figure 1.6). (*Logical/Mathematical and Interpersonal Intelligences*)

Desert	Means of Formation
Sahara	Prevailing Winds
Great Basin Desert	Mountain Blockage

➤ Figure 1.6. Desert Formation

➤ Activity Plan 3: Desert Discovery Centers

Materials

Construction paper (selection of colors)

Cardboard geometric shapes (Browse the pages of the book to create template patterns in cardboard; students will use the templates to trace shapes for the pictures they want to create.)

Scissors (Be sure to remind students about safety rules for using scissors.)

Glue

Long sheet of butcher paper that can become the petroglyph mural (Find a wall for its display and be sure to hang it so students can reach it and attach their shape pictures without too much difficulty; see figure 1.7.)

Large, shallow container of sand (or a sand table)

Variety of materials (cotton, twigs, etc.) for creating the desert habitat

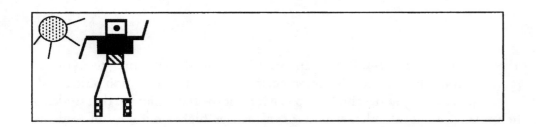

➤ Figure 1.7. Petroglyph Mural

Engage

Display some of the items that will be used in the discovery centers (the cardboard templates for the art project and the miscellaneous materials that will be used to create the desert habitat).

Elaborate

Introduce the discovery center activities and explain the products that will be required:

1. Stand in front of the petroglyph mural as you introduce the shapes and more shapes center. Tell the students: Ancient tribes made petroglyph drawings on the walls of the canyons where they lived. In this center we will be creating our own petroglyph story. As you begin, look through the book (*Arrow to the Sun*) once again, then examine the cardboard template shapes to imagine the picture you would like to create. Use the cardboard shapes as your patterns for tracing and create the shapes you need from the construction paper supplies in the center. Glue the shapes into the picture you imagine, sign your artwork, then attach it to this mural paper.

2. Walk to the sand table (or a large shallow container of sand), dip your hand into the sand, and let the sand dribble through your fingers back into the container. Tell the students: Sand is the main ingredient of the desert and it can be molded into dunes and gentle hills. In the desert habitat center your job will be to add an animal, a plant, or a land formation that might be found in the desert; eventually, when everyone has completed this center, our sand table will look like a desert habitat.

3. Ask the students: If you were a plant or an animal that lived in the desert, what survival abilities would you need? (ways to live in the hot sun and the cool nights and without a lot of water, food sources, and protection from enemies) In the center you will see a list of animals and plants of the desert; your job is to choose one and create an adaptation poster that shows how the animal handles sunny days and cool nights, uses water, finds food, and protects itself from enemies.

Explore

Divide the class into three teams. Have team one start at the shapes center, team two at the desert habitat center, and team three at the adaptation poster center. The adaptation posters will require a visit to the library for research on the chosen topic. Monitor the traffic flow so that students do not overcrowd the centers; usually the shapes center can manage higher numbers of students working at once. Encourage thoughtful, careful work at each center.

Connect

At the end of each afternoon of work, have students share products they have finished, then reflect on work that still needs completing.

SHAPES AND MORE SHAPES

Produce a picture based on the ideas in the story. Use the construction paper in the center and trace the template patterns or create your own shapes and patterns. Cut out the construction paper shapes and assemble the shapes into a picture representing an idea from the story. Display your finished picture on the petroglyph mural; be sure to sign your picture. (*Visual/Spatial Intelligence*)

A DESERT HABITAT

Help build a desert habitat. Investigate plants, animals, and land forms of the desert and use supplies in the center to make a plant, an animal, or a land form for the desert habitat. Carefully add your contribution to the sand table; be sure not to disturb the work of another student. (*Bodily/Kinesthetic Intelligence*)

ADAPTING TO THE LAND

We have learned that deserts have very little water and are usually very hot during the day and very cool in the night; plants and animals that can survive in this environment have adapted to the lack of water and the extremes in temperature. They have also found ways to protect themselves from enemies and to find food for survival. (*Visual/Spatial and Verbal/Linguistic Intelligences*)

1. Choose a plant or animal of the desert from among the following: saguaro cactus, barrel cactus, yucca, carpet of snow, Mexican poppy, desert tortoise, kangaroo rat, desert horned toad, antelope squirrel, gila woodpecker, elf owl, pack rat, pocket mouse, badger, sand lizard, roadrunner, greasewood plant, buzzard, gopher, rattlesnake, Joshua tree, chuckwalla, or desert iguana.

2. Begin the poster by drawing and coloring a large picture of the animal.

3. Find out about the plant or animal, then write first-person adaptation statements that tell how the plant or animal has adapted to the desert environment.

4. If you are stumped for ideas, look at the adaptations of the camel and the lizard.

Camel's Adaptations

I use my humps to store fat, which can be used for water.

I have two-toed feet that spread out as I walk. This stops me from sinking into the sand.

I have bushy eyebrows and two rows of eyelashes. These help keep sand out of my eyes.

I have slits for my nose, these close and also keep sand out of my nose.

My powerful teeth help me get and eat all kinds of plants and twigs.

Adaptations of the Fringe-toed Lizard

I have excellent eyesight and a good sense of smell. These help keep me safe and help me find food.

Special scales on my eyes keep sand out of my eyes.

My tail is fragile and will break off when I am caught. The tail I lose will continue to move and wiggle after I lose it. This distracts my enemy and I can often scurry away. I will grow a new tail, but it will be shorter.

Scales that stick out on the sides of my toes keep me from sinking into the sand.

My nose is shovel-shaped. It helps me dig a path when I dive into the sand.

➤ Culminating Activity Plan: Problem Solving

Engage

Have students use the steps of the creative problem-solving process to investigate and select animals that might also perform the work of the camel. (*Logical/Mathematical Intelligence*)

Sensing the Problem

The camel is used widely throughout desert areas; however, there are not enough camels for all the people who need them. Ask the students: What other animal might adapt to life in the desert and could be used for the purposes of the camel? (Some answers may be llama, burro, donkey, ostrich, and horse. Record these ideas on the board.)

Fact Finding

Ask students what information you need to make this decision. (Some answers may be a description of the camel and the adaptations it has made to surviving in the desert, an investigation of other animals that have similar characteristics, or an exploration of other animals who are included in the family of camels. Give students sufficient time to research these questions.) Tell students to take three sheets of chart paper and label the first, adaptations of camels; the second, other animals in the family of camels; and the third, adaptations of other animals. As students complete their research, have them record the information they find on the appropriate charts.

Explore

Problem Finding

Ask the students: What is the problem we are trying to solve? (There is a shortage of camels for the work that is needed; are there other animals that can be substituted for the camel?) What is the question we are trying to answer? Have students brainstorm questions and select the one that most closely matches this one: What other animal might successfully complete the work of the camel in the desert environment?

Connect

Idea Finding

Review the chart information and list the animals that might substitute for the camel.

Acceptance Finding

Have students work with partners to design advertising brochures selling the merits of this new animal of the desert. (*Visual/Spatial, Verbal/Linguistic, and Interpersonal Intelligences*)

Solution Finding

Brainstorm criteria to judge the ideas. (Examples: water needs, coat, eyes, nose, feet, personality, trainability, endurance.) Create a solution grid (see figure 1.8) listing five animals down the side of the grid. Across the top of the grid, list the criteria. Rate each animal's effectiveness using the criteria. A score of 5 means the animal is very well suited for the desert. A score of 1 means the animal is not at all suited for the desert. The animal with the highest score is the one that would be most acceptable.

ANIMALS	Water Needs	Strength/ Endurance	Coat	Feet	Eyes	Nose	Can Be Trained	TOTALS
Llama								
Burro								
Donkey								
Ostrich								
Horse								

➤ **Figure 1.8. Solution Finding Grid**

2 The Girl Who Loved Wild Horses

Written by Paul Goble

Illustrated by Paul Goble

Scarsdale, NY: Bradbury Press, 1978

Summary

➤ This is a thoughtful story about a young girl's special understanding of horses. The horses follow her to drink at the river and in the hot sun she sleeps contentedly beside them as they graze among the flowers near her village. Suddenly, a storm stampedes the horses and the girl finds herself alone in a distant land; she is not afraid because she and the horses of the village are befriended by a beautiful spotted stallion. A year later she returns to her people but she is not content; her parents agree that she should go back to live with the wild horses.

Award Year

➤ 1979

Art Information

➤ Illustrated using water colors and pen and ink.

Curriculum Connections

➤ Native American culture groups (Plains, Eastern Woodlands, Desert Southwest, Pacific Northwest)

➤ Activity Plan 1: Sharing the Story

Materials

Caldecott Award poster
Watercolor paints (available at art stores)
Pen and ink (available at art stores)

Engage

Explore the movement of the buffalo. Have students demonstrate how buffalo might behave in warm sunshine (basking), how they might react to a storm (stampede, become skittery), and what they enjoy after a storm on the plains (wallowing in rain puddles). (*Bodily/Kinesthetic Intelligence*)

Elaborate

An important part of the lifestyle of the Plains Indians was their cycle of following the buffalo herds. Ask the students why buffalo were important to their survival. (List responses on chart paper or the board and save for the end of the lesson; some answers may be food, clothing, tools, and shelter.)

Explore

As students listen to and watch the story, ask them to notice other details or clues to the lifestyle of the Plains Indians. Share the story.

Connect

Share the Caldecott Award information:

1. As students examine the cover of the book, ask them what special thing they notice. (gold medal) Ask them what the name of the medal is. (Caldecott Award Medal) Ask them why it has been placed on this book. (Some answers may be that the illustrations are special, well done, particularly interesting, exciting, and/or unusual.)

2. Discuss the art techniques used in creating the pictures. Ask the students how Mr. Goble's art foreshadows what might happen. (Return to the beginning of the book and slowly turn the pages as you pose the question and wait for responses; students should notice the rolling black clouds of the approaching storm, then the increasing strength of the storm with high winds and lightning strikes.) Another page to examine closely is the one where the scene is mirrored in the water. Ask the students what kind of weather happens in this picture. (clear, hot, sunny day, low humidity) Ask them what other details about the lifestyle of the Plains Indian are evident through the illustrations. (Horses were necessary. Color and

design were used in many ways. In following the cycle of the buffalo, the people experienced many landscape changes.)

3. Ask two student volunteers to search the poster for the year the story won. (Searching the poster helps students become familiar with the different titles selected for the award.)

Food, clothing, tools, and shelter are important uses of the buffalo. Ask students what other information they learned from the story. (Buffalo roamed the prairie lands, hunters followed their migration and killed for the tribe, hides provided teepee coverings and material for clothing, and the bones could be carved into tools and toys.)

Have students use the brainstormed information to write an acrostic poem about the buffalo; acrostic poems describe the topic and use the letters of the topic to begin each line. Divide the class into seven groups, one for each letter of the word, and have student groups use the letters to write descriptive sentences for each line of the poem. (*Verbal/Linguistic Intelligence*)

Buffalo roamed the prairie land,

Under blue skies and stormy clouds they lived.

Fresh meat for the Indians,

From the hides come skins for teepees and clothes,

And from the bones came tools and toys.

Long, long ago, there were lots more buffalo.

Oh, what a wonderful sight they were for the hunters of the Plains.

➤ Activity Plan 2: Exploring the Landscapes of the Plains

Materials

Enlarged map showing the cultural regions of the Native Americans (figure 2.1)
Activity sheet 2.1, Landscape Forms (one per student)
Scraps of paper in different textures and colors (newspaper, construction paper,
    wrapping paper, foil paper, wallpaper samples)
Glue

Engage

Show the map of the United States, and talk about the areas where different tribes lived. *The Girl Who Loved Wild Horses* is an American Indian story. (*Visual/Spatial Intelligence*)

Text continues on page 20.

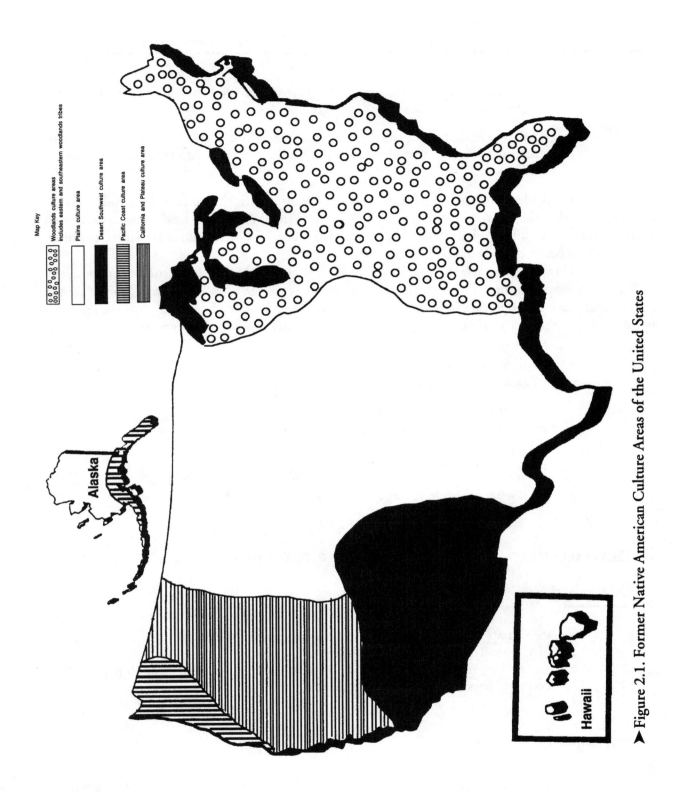

Woodlands culture areas
includes eastern and southeastern woodlands tribes

Plains culture area

Desert Southwest culture area

Pacific Coast culture area

California and Plateau culture area

Alaska

Hawaii

▶ Figure 2.1. Former Native American Culture Areas of the United States

➤Activity Sheet 2.1. Landscape Forms

Elaborate

There are many landscapes represented in the Plains. Ask the students what some of the landscapes are. (Brainstorm land forms found in the book: prairie, river, stream, hill, valley, waterfall, mesa, desert.) (*Verbal/Linguistic Intelligence*)

Explore

Have students work with partners, using the landscape forms (see activity sheet 2.1) to create torn paper landscapes representing those found on the plains. Torn paper pictures should reflect a landscape focus (prairie, river, stream, hill, valley, waterfall, mesa, or desert) and a silhouette of a horse or a buffalo. (*Visual/Spatial Intelligence*)

Connect

Share and display the landscape creations.

➤ Activity Plan 3: Exploring Native American Culture Areas

Materials

Globe

Four long sheets of butcher paper (Students will use these sheets to create murals in the "A Day in the Life" center.)

Enlarged comparison chart (see figure 2.2)

Activity sheet 2.2, Goal Setting (two or three copies per group; to be completed by student groups at the beginning of each day's discovery center work; the sheet helps students identify responsibilities for each member of the group. As you circulate among the groups, you can use it as a checklist and as a way to redirect off-task behaviors; for example, "Mary, share with me the jobs of your group for today. Jerome, what progress have you made in completing your job for the day?")

Various myths and legends from the four culture areas (Consult with the librarian to identify one or two myths and legends from each culture area.)

Culture Areas	Food	Transportation	Homes	Arts/Crafts	Other Interesting Facts
Pacific Northwest					
Desert Southwest					
Plains					
Eastern Woodlands					

➤ **Figure 2.2. Native American Culture Areas**

Engage

Show the map again (see figure 2.1), review the four culture areas, and have students select the culture areas they wish to explore. (*Note:* Depending on your class size, try to create fairly evenly divided groups, so that five to six students work in each culture area.) (*Visual/Spatial Intelligence*)

Background Information

Most historians agree that the Americas were discovered some 30,000 or 40,000 years ago when hunters from Asia crossed to Alaska from Siberia across the Bering Strait. Different groups slowly spread across North America and into South America. Scientists have grouped these early peoples into culture areas according to their ways of obtaining food, building shelter, and living together. Four of the culture areas in North America are the Pacific Northwest, the Desert Southwest, the Plains, and the Eastern Woodlands.

Goal Setting Sheet			Our Culture Area:			
Date	At Home	A Day in the Life	Telling Stories	Entertaining	Comparison Chart	Presentation Plans

▶Activity Sheet 2.2. Goal Setting

The Haida were one people living in the Northwest. Salmon was the mainstay of their diet, but they also ate halibut, trout, herring, shellfish, and even some edible seaweed. When the salmon came upriver to spawn, the Haida built traps and caught and dried enough salmon to feed the tribe for the whole year and have some left for trading. Because of this abundance, the winter months were usually free for resting, woodworking, basket making, and other activities. The Haida used the tall cedar trees that also grow in the Pacific Northwest to build houses. The houses were large enough to hold several families, and division and placement of the living areas within the house were determined by the ranks of the families. A fire pit with a smoke hole in the roof above was built in the center of the house, and outside the house stood a large wooden pole decorated with symbols significant for the important family of the house. Because food was so plentiful, the Haida had time and energy to build a complicated society based on rank and wealth.

The Desert Southwest tribes lived in a very different area than the Pacific Coast, the arid lands of Arizona and New Mexico. The Hopi were a people of this area; they were farmers, growing corn, squash, tobacco, and beans on the flatlands where springs and water runoff from higher grounds could water the crops. The Hopi used stone covered with mud to build houses on easily defended high grounds, and entry to the houses was through a roof opening reached by ladders. The houses faced a central plaza where many religious and community events took place; another important community space was the kiva, located under the central plaza. Hopi men farmed and hunted and led the religious and ceremonial events; Hopi women owned the houses, made the house rules, managed the planting and harvesting, cooked, and made pottery and baskets.

The Pawnee were a tribe of the Plains culture area. They were both farmers and hunters, hunting the buffalo in late spring and fall and planting and harvesting corn, squash, and beans in early spring and late summer. The Pawnee had two houses, the more permanent lodges built of logs, dirt, and grass and the portable teepees made from buffalo skins that were used during the hunt. The Pawnee lived in villages. Several leaders, priests, and men and women worked together to plant and cultivate crops; on the hunt, men were responsible for tracking and killing the buffalo and the women and children assisted.

The Iroquois nation's peoples lived in the food-rich Eastern Woodlands where game was plentiful (deer, beaver, turkey, fish, duck, geese) and farming was easy (squash, many kinds of corn and beans). They also ate nuts and fruits and learned to tap the maple trees for syrup. Villages were built along riverbanks and surrounded with fences made from wooden posts. Within the villages many families lived together in longhouses, which were 50 to 150 feet in length. To stop war among the nations and to protect themselves from enemies, the five major nations speaking the Iroquois language formed a league, with each nation governing itself through a council.

Elaborate

Introduce the discovery centers and describe the expectations for each center using the following narration:

A long, long time ago, long before Columbus sailed on his historic voyage, hunters from Asia crossed to Alaska from Siberia across the Bering Strait. [Show this on the globe.] Different groups continued to travel across this land bridge and slowly spread across North America and into South America. Scientists have grouped these early peoples into culture areas according to their ways of obtaining food, building shelter, and living together.

Four of the projects ask you to discover and show the customs and traditions of each culture area. In the "At Home" center, you will build homes that show the style of shelters the people in your culture area built. "A Day in the Life" is a mural you will create that illustrates foods, transportation methods, fun and games, and the organization of the shelters. Everyone in the group will need to contribute to the mural. A pictograph dictionary and a story told through the pictograph will be the required products from the "Telling Stories" center; two members of the group will want to partner to work on this activity. In the "Entertainment" center, one member of the group will research the culture group's customs in music and musical instruments, create a musical instrument, and demonstrate its use. When you have completed your research and these four activities, work together as a group to design a creative way to share what you have learned; also, complete the comparison chart (figure 2.2) to help the class see at a glance the differences and similarities among the culture areas.

Our final project will be designing and making "dream catchers." Dream catchers were gifts to newborn children that hung above or from the cradle boards of the babies. The purpose of a dream catcher was to catch bad dreams in the web (bad dreams were believed to have rough edges that would easily catch in the web) and only allow good dreams or dreams blessed with love through to the sleeping child. Dream catcher webs (like a spider's web) were formed on small hoops made from grapevine or ash or hickory strips; rawhide strips, horsehair, hemp, and even yarn. The webs could be decorated with beads and feathers and soft fur.

Explore

Have students meet in their culture groups, select assignments, and begin to work. Circulate as students research and prepare their products to encourage and support contributions from each member in the group, assist in locating resources and completing research, and help students think about "found" rather than "purchased" materials as they create the required products. (*Interpersonal Intelligence*)

Allow significant blocks of time each day for the discovery center work; completion of the products and preparation for the presentation takes at least a week and really needs two weeks. An effective routine for each day's discovery center work would be as follows:

1. Begin by sharing and briefly discussing a legend or myth from the four culture areas; this expands and enriches students' awareness of the customs and traditions of Native Americans.

2. Continue with goal setting by each group (have students use activity sheet 2.2); setting goals helps students with their organization and productivity skills and reinforces an important component of collaborative projects—that each student in the collaborative group contribute significantly to the work of the group. Require that students be very specific as they complete the goal setting sheet for each day of work (see figure 2.3).

3. End with reflection time. Have students reflect on their daily accomplishments by responding to these questions: What did I do? Why did I do it? What did I learn? Daily reflection helps students see progress in reaching daily goals (and lack of progress for those students who struggled with focus and accomplishment). Reflection also assists students in setting new goals for the coming day's work.

4. Devote one block of time to the Creating Dream Catchers center and have students design, create, and share their dream catchers.

Date	At Home	A Day in the Life	Telling Stories	Entertaining	Comparison Chart	Presentation Plans
Tuesday	Len will begin building the shelter and Natasha will revise and publish the paragraph about the shelter.	Mary will draw and color the scene on the mural showing ways the people of the cultural area traveled.	Jerome will finish coloring the dictionary pictograph while Mary works on the mural.	Latoya will revise and publish the paragraph about the musical instrument and continue to practice playing the instrument.	Natasha will summarize the shelter information and Mary will write the information about the ways the people of the area traveled.	We are not ready to begin planning how we will share with the class.

➤ Figure 2.3. Daily Goal Setting

Connect

Have student groups present to the class and other guests.

AT HOME

Build a home that represents how the Native Americans of your culture area lived. Write a paragraph explaining why this was the kind of home that was built in your culture area. Be sure to include a topic sentence, three or four supporting detail sentences, and a closing sentence in your paragraph. (*Bodily/Kinesthetic Intelligence*)

A DAY IN THE LIFE

Create a mural showing a day in the life of a Native American from your culture area. Show transportation, food, recreation, and the setting of a village. Write captions that explain why the Native Americans of this culture area used this kind of transportation, ate these kinds of foods, participated in these kinds of games and fun, and organized their villages in this way. (*Visual/Spatial Intelligence*)

TELLING STORIES

Create a pictograph dictionary. Write a story using the symbols in your pictograph dictionary. Investigate the languages of your culture area and write a paragraph about them. (*Verbal/Linguistic Intelligence*)

ENTERTAINING

Make an instrument that would have been played in your culture area. Show the class how the instrument is played. Write a paragraph explaining why this was an instrument of your culture area. Be sure to include a topic sentence, three or four supporting detail sentences, and a closing sentence in your paragraph. (*Musical/Rhythmic Intelligence*)

COMPARING CULTURAL AREAS

Use the class comparison chart to list the required information: homes, foods, transportation, arts and crafts, and other interesting facts. Be sure you can explain why these are typical of your culture area. (*Logical/Mathematical Intelligence*)

PRESENTING WHAT WE LEARNED

Work with your team to design and practice a creative way to share what you have learned about the Native Americans of your culture area. (*Interpersonal Intelligence*)

CREATING DREAM CATCHERS

Design and create a dream catcher. Dream catchers were gifts to new-born children that hung above or from the cradle boards of the babies. The purpose of a dream catcher was to catch bad dreams in the web (bad dreams were believed to have rough edges that would easily catch in the web) and only allow good dreams or dreams blessed with love through to the sleeping child. Dream catcher webs (like a spider's web) were formed on small hoops made from grapevine or ash or hickory strips; rawhide strips, horsehair, hemp, and even yarn. The webs could be decorated with beads and feathers and soft fur or other treasures meaningful to the family. (*Intrapersonal Intelligence*)

3 The Glorious Flight: Across the Channel with Louis Blériot

Written by Alice Provensen and Martin Provensen

Illustrated by Alice Provensen and Martin Provensen

New York: Viking Press, 1983

Summary

➤ When Louis Blériot catches sight of an airship flying over the city of Cambrai, France in 1901, he has only one wish: "I, too, will build a flying machine, a great white bird. We will work hard. We will all fly through the air like swallows!" He begins to invent but his first flying ship is too small and its wings flap like a chicken's; his second is a glider large enough for a man, but it never takes off; he adds a motor and a propeller in his third, but it still won't take off. Success comes with his eleventh invention!

Award Year

➤ 1984

Art Information

➤ Illustrated using acrylics and pen and ink.

Curriculum Connections

➤ Biographies of people who have made a difference, flight

➤ Activity Plan 1: Sharing the Story

Materials

Pictures of famous people, some familiar and some not so familiar (An easy way to collect pictures is to select a variety of biographies that have portraits on their covers, e.g., biographies about presidents, explorers, musicians, inventors, artists, athletes, human rights activists.)

Biographies (one per student) (You may want to precede this presentation of *The Glorious Flight* with the biography introductory lesson, page 33; the lesson includes a trip to the library to select biographies for independent reading.)

Activity sheet, 3.1, Monsieur Blériot's Inventions Chart (Make a transparency of it, or enlarge it so it can seen by the whole class.)

Timeline. Using a twenty-foot, ten-inch sheet of butcher paper, create a long black line and divide the line into ten-inch increments; mark the lines in twenty-five-year divisions, starting with 1400 (see figure 3.1).

Caldecott Award poster

Pen and ink (available at art stores)

Acrylic paint (available at art stores)

```
1400  1425                                           1975  2000
```

➤ Figure 3.1. Biography Timeline

Engage

Show pictures of people from the selected biographies and ask students to identify why they are worth remembering.

Elaborate

Introduce *The Glorious Flight*. Explain that this is a story about a pioneer in aviation. Ask students to notice how many flying machines Blériot creates until one actually flies, to identify the problems he faces with each new invention, and to describe what inspires him to try again.

Explore

Read the story.

Monsieur Bleriot's Inventions and What Happens!
Bleriot I:
Bleriot II:
Bleriot III:
Bleriot IV:
Bleriot V :
Bleriot VI:
Bleriot VII:
Bleriot VIII —Bleriot X :
Bleriot XI:

➤ Activity Sheet 3.1. Monsieur Blériot's Inventions Chart

Connect

Ask the students how many flying machines Mr. Blériot invented. (eleven) Show the inventions chart after the students identify the number (activity sheet 3.1). Ask them to name some of the problems he faced. (Use the chart to make notes as the students give responses. Sample responses follow.)

Blériot I: too small, wings flap like a chicken

Blériot II: glider, large enough for a man, never takes off

Blériot III: adds a motor and a propeller, won't take off

Blériot IV: two motors, two propellers, goes in circles

Blériot V: hops like a rabbit

Blériot VI: sails across a field, hits a rock

Blériot VII: flies, but eventually crashes

Blériot VIII–Blériot X: don't know about these

Blériot XI: flies! success

Monsieur Blériot kept trying and trying to invent a flying machine. Ask the students: What kept him going? Why did he keep trying? What words would you use to describe people who make a difference?

Roll out the timeline. Address the students as follows:

We have just learned about Monsieur Blériot, a person who made a difference in the history of flying. How would you describe his accomplishments? [Built eleven machines; worked many years; kept trying over and over; wasn't afraid.] Let's write those accomplishments in couplet form; a couplet has two lines of writing, the end words rhyme, and each line has the same number of syllables. [See figure 3.2 for a sample couplet.] Where shall we place it on the timeline? [1901–1909] Let's add an illustration to the couplet. [We drew a picture of one of his flying machines.] We will add other couplets and pictures as you finish your biographies.

Monsieur Bleriot was a flying pioneer.
Eleven machines he built, never showing fear!

➤ Figure 3.2. Timeline Couplet

Share the Caldecott Award information:

1. As students examine the cover of the book, ask them what special thing they notice. (gold medal) Ask them what the name of the medal is. (Caldecott Award Medal) Ask them why it has been placed on this book. (Some answers may be that the illustrations are special, well done, particularly interesting, exciting, and/or unusual.)

2. Discuss the art techniques used in creating the pictures. Details, color, and perspective are very noticeable in the illustrations created by the Provensens.

   - *The dinner table scene (page 5)*: Point out the table setting and the richness of Mama's dress. Ask students how they would describe the location of the home. (There is a sense of height, living above the city.)

   - *The city streets (pages 6–11)*: Point out the windows, doors and buildings.

   - *The first view of the airship (pages 12–13)*: The perspective is unusual.

   - *The flight of Blériot IV (page 21)*: Point out the sense of movement as the illustrators reinforce the text, that is, this flying ship went in "beautiful circles." Ask the students how the illustrators create the feeling of movement. (the swirl of the water and the background)

   - *The change in perspective (pages 30–37)*: Point out the change in perspective as the reader now joins Blériot in the suspenseful trip across the Channel, as the French coast disappears and the fog encircles the plane.

   - *Media*: The Provensens used pen and ink and acrylic paints to create the illustrations. Each illustration looks like a full-color painting that could stand alone on a wall.

3. Ask two student volunteers to search the poster for the year the story won. (Searching the poster helps students become familiar with the many titles selected for the award.)

➤ Activity Plan 2: Introducing Biographies

Materials

Preplanning with the librarian (Students will be selecting biographies for independent reading; the librarian can booktalk suggested titles or allow the students to browse.)
Examples: a biography and an encyclopedia article about the same person

Engage

Make a web diagram on the board and write *bio* = and *graphy* = in the center circle (see figure 3.3).

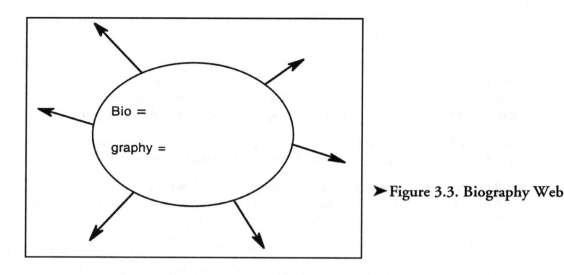

➤ Figure 3.3. Biography Web

Ask students questions to identify meanings for these two words:

1. What does the prefix "bio" mean? Refocus question: What are you studying if you take a course in biology? "Bio" means life. (Add this information to the circle. See figure 3.4.)

2. What is the meaning of "graphy?" Refocus question: Think of words like *geography* and *photography*. Now can you identify the meaning? "Graphy" means recording. (Add this definition to the circle. See figure 3.4.) A biography is a recording or story of the life of a person. (Write this definition above the diagram; see figure 3.4.)

Elaborate

Show and read a little from the encyclopedia article about a person and the biography about the person. Ask students how a biography is different from an encyclopedia article.

Add students' responses to the web (see figure 3.4). Responses may include provides *more details* and is more *personal* (home life, beliefs, feelings and emotions), usually has conversations, describes obstacles/challenges the people faced, gives us an understanding of the times in which the people lived, explains experiences that really made a difference in their lives, illustrates facts/details about childhood experiences, and explains more about the events that made them famous.

There are different kinds of biographies: *authentic biographies* are well-documented and researched and include real photographs and actual conversations involving the person; *fictionalized biographies* also show careful research, but the author may dramatize certain events and invent the conversations that happen in these events; *autobiographies and memoirs* are written by the person they are about.

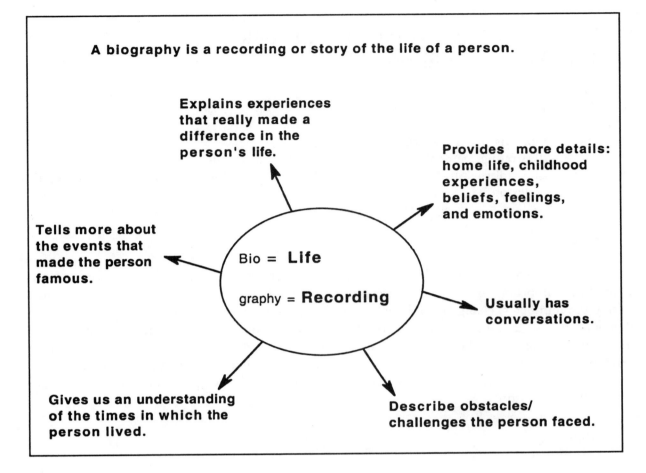

A biography is a recording or story of the life of a person.

Explains experiences that really made a difference in the person's life.

Provides more details: home life, childhood experiences, beliefs, feelings, and emotions.

Tells more about the events that made the person famous.

Bio = **Life**

graphy = **Recording**

Usually has conversations.

Gives us an understanding of the times in which the person lived.

Describe obstacles/ challenges the person faced.

➤ Figure 3.4. Completed Biography Web

Explore

Tell the students: In a little while you will be selecting a biography in the library. Think about a person you might like to discover through your reading. (Go to the library and give students time to browse and select biographies for independent reading.)

Connect

Assign the students this question to answer as they read: From the title and the cover and jacket words and illustrations, what do you think you will say about how this person has made a difference in the world? (Allow thinking time, then ask students to share their ideas.) Encourage students to read silently for a while to confirm or change their predictions.

➤ Activity Plan 3: Writing About People Who Make a Difference

Materials

Drawing paper (two sheets per student)
Illustrating materials (crayons, markers, colored pencils)
Biographies (Students should be finished with their biographies before beginning this lesson.)

Engage

Begin with this challenging "quick think" idea: Using the number 7, change it to draw something important about the characters in the biographies you are reading. Refocus statement: Using the number 7, change it to draw how your biography characters are famous. What are they known for? (For example, the seven could become an American flag for George Washington or a helicopter propeller from Leonardo da Vinci's sketches or a medicine jar for Clara Barton, the nurse.) Encourage students to be imaginative; the goal of a "quick think" is to awaken the brain and get it ready for the lesson that follows. Circulate to encourage and support, but resist the temptation to give further directions.

Elaborate

Select a student volunteer and use his or her interests, qualities, and family information to model creating character webs. Before asking for suggestions, emphasize that it is important to choose compliments and "kind" facts rather than make negative statements. Use figure 3.5 as a guide for your own questioning strategies. (For example, if students are stumped about relationships, a question you might ask is, "Who are all the important people in your life?" For qualities, the student who has been chosen may also wish to volunteer information. For interests, refocus questions such as, "How do you spend your week?" or "What activities are really enjoyable to you?" may elicit more responses.)

Explore

Display the Einstein web (figure 3.5) as a model, and have students use the drawing paper to create character webs for the main characters in their biographies. Circulate to model how to use the biographies to find in-depth information.

Connect

Have students share pieces of their webs—qualities, interests, or relationships—then work with partners to analyze the web information for the most important details about their characters.

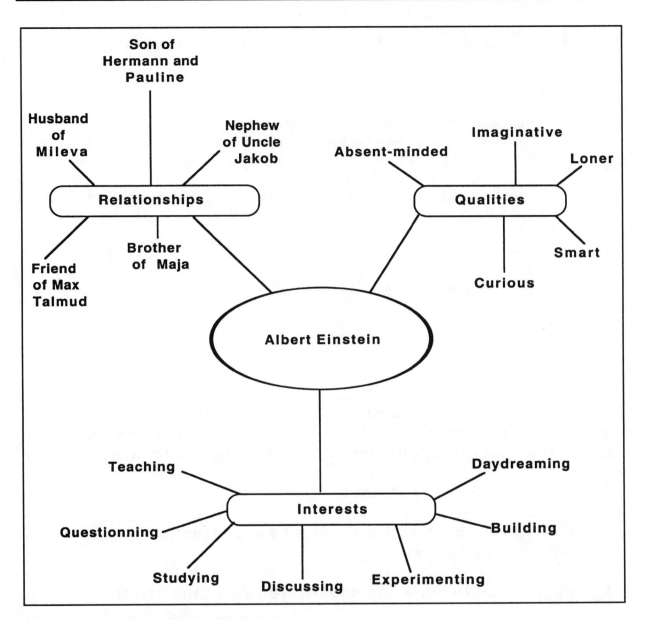

➤ Figure 3.5. Biography Web for Albert Einstein

Give the following directions for writing couplets: Use the important details from the web in writing the two lines of poetry, be sure your end words rhyme, and count the syllables so each line has an equal number of syllables. Circulate to help count syllables and create rhyming end words. Once couplets are revised and edited, students should print or type them, glue them to the timeline, and prepare accompanying illustrations.

➤ Activity Plan 4: Exploring Gravity and Movement

Materials

Large baggy (one per student) containing:
- cardboard shape with five nail holes poked near the perimeter (See figure 3.6.)
- nail with a head, at least two inches in length (*Note:* Caution students to work carefully as they use the nail.)
- twelve-inch length of yarn, one end tied with a small weight, the other end tied in a loop
- directions for the experiment (See figure 3.7.)

Pencils
Book
Heavy load (Books in a carryall container will work.)

➤ Figure 3.6.
Cardboard Shape

Finding the Center of Gravity

1. **Push a nail through one of the holes in the cardboard.**

2. **Hang a weight from the nail.**

3. **Let the cardboard and the weight swing freely. They will soon come to rest.**

4. **Use a pencil to mark the downward line of the string.**

5. **Repeat in each hole.**

6. **The point where the five lines meet is the center of weight or gravity.**

7. **Draw a circle at the center of gravity and use the nail head to balance the cardboard shape.**

➤ Figure 3.7. Center of Gravity Experiment Directions

Engage

Explore flight movements with the students: soar (like Blériot 11); zoom (like a jet today); whir (Ask students: What kind of flying machine whirs?); sail (like Blériot 6); glide (like Blériot 2); flit, flutter (like Blériot 1); drift, hover (like Blériot 3); swarm, float (like Blériot 7); hop (like Blériot 5). (*Bodily/Kinesthetic Intelligence*)

Elaborate

Instruct the students as follows: An important consideration in the flight of an airplane is the center of gravity or the center of weight. Airplanes carefully place people and baggage so that the weight is carefully balanced. Let's experiment with this today (*Bodily/Kinesthetic Intelligence*):

1. Stand with both feet on the ground; your feet should be pressed closely together; move your feet so they are comfortably apart. Which gives better balance? Why?

2. Stand with your arms pressed closely to your sides and balance on one foot; try again, using your arms as needed. Which gives better balance? Why?

3. What happens when you carry a heavy load in one arm? (Ask a volunteer to pick up a bag filled with books and walk across the room. Repeat as needed.) Have students describe what they observe and explain why.

4. Place a book on a table and slowly push it toward the edge until it falls off the table. Repeat slowly to find the center of balance. Why is this important in loading an airliner?

Explore

Have students explore finding the center of gravity. They should work with partners and take turns finding the centers of gravity in the cardboard shapes; one student holds the nail, the other student hangs the weight and marks the line of the string.

Give students a copy of figure 3.7 and have them read the directions.

Connect

Have the students experiment with adding baggage to the cardboard shape by taping a small object to one side. Ask them what is needed to provide a counterbalance. Discuss what students have learned and make generalizations; some answers may be:

1. The center of gravity is the line or point where the object is evenly balanced.

2. A plane needs an evenly balanced load to fly.

3. If the load is out of balance, the wings or the nose or tail will tip and the plane will not fly.

➤Activity Plan 5: Lighter Than Air—Hot-Air Balloons

Materials

Bottle with a small neck
Balloon (Inflate the balloon; tie it, and attach a string to it. Poke the string into the
    neck of the bottle until the balloon is resting on the bottle's neck; see figure 3.8.)
Hot water from the sink
Dry cleaner plastic bags (one per small group)
Transparent tape (one roll per small group)
Staplers (one per small group)
Scissors (One pair per student; be sure to review scissors safety rules with the students.)
Hot air popcorn popper or a portable hair dryer

➤Figure 3.8. Hot Air Rises
Demonstration

← Water level

Engage

Ask the students: What will happen to the balloon if we partially fill this bottle with hot, hot water? (Allow speculation, then fill the bottle halfway with hot water from the sink and watch what happens; as heat expands the air and increases the pressure around the balloon, the balloon stands up.)

Elaborate

Tell the students about the history of hot-air ballooning:

More than twenty-five years before Monsieur Blériot flew across the English Channel, two other Frenchmen, the Montgolfier brothers, experimented with hot air and balloons made from linen and paper and successfully launched a hot-air balloon in 1783. Because they knew that hot air was lighter than cold air, they built a fire under the balloon and watched it rise. Eventually, they attached a basket carrier to the balloon and two passengers standing in the basket lifted into the sky as the balloon filled with hot air.

Explore

Have students work in small groups to shape and design the dry cleaner bags into hot-air balloons (using scissors, tape, and the stapler) and test their designs. Do the following to test the flight of the balloons:

1. Have the small group of students center the plastic bag over the corn popper or the hair dryer. Each member of the group should retain a hold on the bag to keep it open and keep it from lifting.

2. Turn on the popper or the dryer and let the balloon fill with warm air.

3. Have students decide the signal and the timing for releasing the balloon.

4. Let them release the balloon and watch its flight.

Repeat the process until all the groups have tested their balloon designs. Then ask them which balloon flew the highest. Discuss and analyze its design to identify the factors that produced this kind of flight.

Connect

Have students make changes in their hot-air balloon designs and test the new designs (using the same process). Ask them to identify what differences (if any) occurred in these flights, which design flew to a greater height, and why.

➤ Activity Plan 6: Air and Lift

Materials

Strips of paper measuring one inch by six inches
Paper (one or two sheets per student; students will use the paper to design and fly paper airplanes; typing paper, construction paper, or drawing paper will work.)

Engage

Distribute the strips of paper. Have students hold one end between their thumbs and first fingers and let the other end dangle across the backs of their hands, then rest the knuckles of their thumbs against their chins, just below their bottom lips. Tell them to blow straight across the papers. As students blow the papers should rise so that they are almost horizontal.

Elaborate

Explain Bernoulli's Principle to the students as follows:

This demonstration illustrates a discovery made by Daniel Bernoulli, a Swiss scientist, which became known as Bernoulli's principle. Seventy-one years before Monsieur Blériot flew in 1909, Bernoulli discovered that moving air has less pressure than the still air around it; this discovery was important for flight because it is the moving air passing over the wings of an airplane that creates lift for the plane. During takeoff the faster an airplane moves through the air, the greater the force of lift.

Tell the students to examine the shape of the wings in Monsieur Blériot's plane that finally flew across the Channel. The top of the wing has a gentle curve and the bottom of the wing is flat (see figure 3.9).

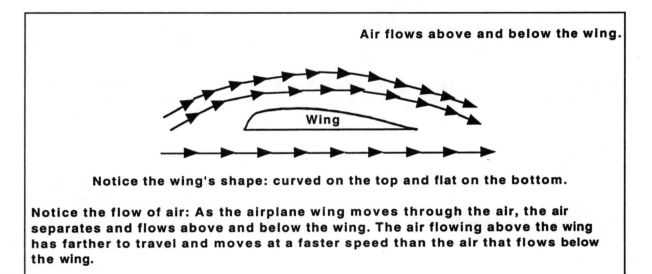

Air flows above and below the wing.

Wing

Notice the wing's shape: curved on the top and flat on the bottom.

Notice the flow of air: As the airplane wing moves through the air, the air separates and flows above and below the wing. The air flowing above the wing has farther to travel and moves at a faster speed than the air that flows below the wing.

➤ Figure 3.9. Airplane Wing Design

This design also supports Bernoulli's principle, because when the wind hits the front edge of the wing, it separates and some travels over the top surface of the wing while the rest travels along the lower surface. Because the air over the top surface of the wing is moving faster than the air on the lower surface, the pressure is lower above the wing than below the wing. The greater pressure from below makes the wing lift.

Explore

Have students use the paper to design paper airplanes, then test the flight capabilities of their designs. Experiment with different ways of releasing the paper airplanes. Ask the students which method produces the greatest distance, the most height, and the most unusual path.

Connect

Have students use the experiments with the cardboard shapes (center of gravity), the hot-air balloons (warm air rises), and the paper airplanes (Bernoulli's principle of lift) to identify the challenges Monsieur Blériot faced in designing an airplane that would fly. Some responses may be:

1. Monsieur Blériot must consider the center of gravity when he designs a plane and expects to employ a human pilot; otherwise the plane will tilt and crash.

2. Monsieur Blériot must find a way to add speed to his plane so that lift takes place.

3. Monsieur Blériot must design the wings so they support Bernoulli's principle for creating lift.

➤ Culminating Activity Plan: Go Fly a Kite

Plan a kite flying day. Students can bring kites from home or make simple kites at school. Norma Dixon's book, *Kites* (New York: Morrow Junior Books, 1996) has some great suggestions and most are made from readily available materials. Try her Bermuda children's kite (a large leaf-design kite made from paper grocery bags) or the flexible kite (looks like a parachute and is made from a plastic garbage bag). Possibly, the only things you will need to purchase are the lightweight wood spines and spars, which are available at most hobby and craft stores, and the parachute kite doesn't even require this.

4 Grandfather's Journey

Written by Allen Say
Illustrated by Allen Say
Boston: Houghton Mifflin, 1993

Summary

➤ Allen Say shares memories of his grandfather's life in America and Japan and conveys his own love for his two countries. His grandfather was a young man when he left Japan to travel through America and settle in San Francisco; but after many years in America he longed to see his homeland again and returned to Japan, where "once again he exchanged stories and laughed with his old friends." Allen Say was born in Japan; when he was nearly grown, he also left home and traveled to California. Like his grandfather, he feels torn between the two countries; when in one country, he invariably misses the other.

Award Year

➤ 1994

Art Information

➤ Illustrated using water colors.

Curriculum Connections

➤ Family heritage

➤ Activity Plan 1: Sharing the Story

Materials

Colorful dot labels
Caldecott Award poster
Watercolor paints (available at art stores)

Engage

Using a laminated map of the world and colorful dot labels, identify and show the birthplaces of the students in the class. Ask them how many of them still live in the town where they were born and what special memories they have about their grandfathers. (*Logical/Mathematical and Visual/Spatial Intelligences*)

Elaborate

Read the story.

Connect

Use what Allen Say shared about his grandfather and the guidelines for writing a bio-poem to model writing a poem about Grandfather. Ask the students for the information needed:

Line 1: Who is Allen Say remembering? (his grandfather)

Line 2: What do we know about Grandfather from the story? (he came to the United States; he traveled a lot; he enjoyed new experiences) What adjectives would summarize those events? (explorer, adventurer, risk-taker)

Line 3: What is his relationship with Allen Say? (his grandfather)

Line 4: What activities, hobbies, and/or jobs are special to Grandfather? (travel, his songbirds, telling stories, laughing with old friends)

Line 5: What do we know about how he feels about his new home in America? (likes living in America, particularly California with its strong sunlight, the Sierra Mountains, and the lonely seacoast) How does he feel about Japan? (misses his home in Japan, the friends, and the mountains and rivers)

Line 6: What is Grandfather's wish near the end of the story? (to see California one last time)

Line 7: Where has Grandfather lived? (San Francisco, California, and a small village in Japan)

Line 8: What is Grandfather's last name? (Say)

The poem might look like this:
Grandfather
Explorer, adventurer
Relative of Allen Say, his grandson, who understands his feeling of homesickness.
Who likes to travel and surrounds himself with songbirds,
Who feels strongly about his adopted home,
Who would like to see California one last time,
Resident of San Francisco, California and a small village in Japan,
Say

Connect

Ask the students what Allen Say means when he says at the end of the story, "I think I know my grandfather now." Ask them what special memories they have of times with favorite relatives. Share the Caldecott Award information:

1. As students examine the cover of the book, ask them what special thing they notice? (gold medal) Ask them what the name of the medal is. (Caldecott Award Medal) Ask them why it has been placed on this book. (Some answers may be that the illustrations are special, well done, particularly interesting, exciting, and/or unusual.)

2. Discuss the art technique used in creating the pictures. Watercolor is the medium for the illustrations in this story, and each illustration is like a painting that could stand alone. Browse the pictures to show the variety of water textures as Grandfather crosses the ocean and explores America (pages 5–6, 13–15, and 19). The desert illustration (page 8) really shows the watercolor technique in the shadings of deep pinks and purples to pale pinks and purples. The perspective of that page also really emphasizes the size of the rocks. Ask the students if they can find Grandfather. Another spectacular landscape scene is the California seacoast (page 14), from the deep purple of the foreground cliffs to the haziness in the far background cliffs. The illustrations showing Grandfather's return to Japan reinforce why he returned and what he missed: the mountains, the rivers, the gardens, and the flowering trees (see the illustrations starting on page 20).

3. Ask two student volunteers to search the poster for the year the story won. (Searching the poster helps students become familiar with the many different titles selected for the award.)

➤ Activity Plan 2: My Favorite Relative

Materials

Activity sheet 4.1, Interview Web (one per student)
Activity sheet 4.2, Bio-poem Directions (one per student)
Transparency of the bio-poem the class wrote about Grandfather (from the "Sharing the Story" lesson)

Text continues on page 50.

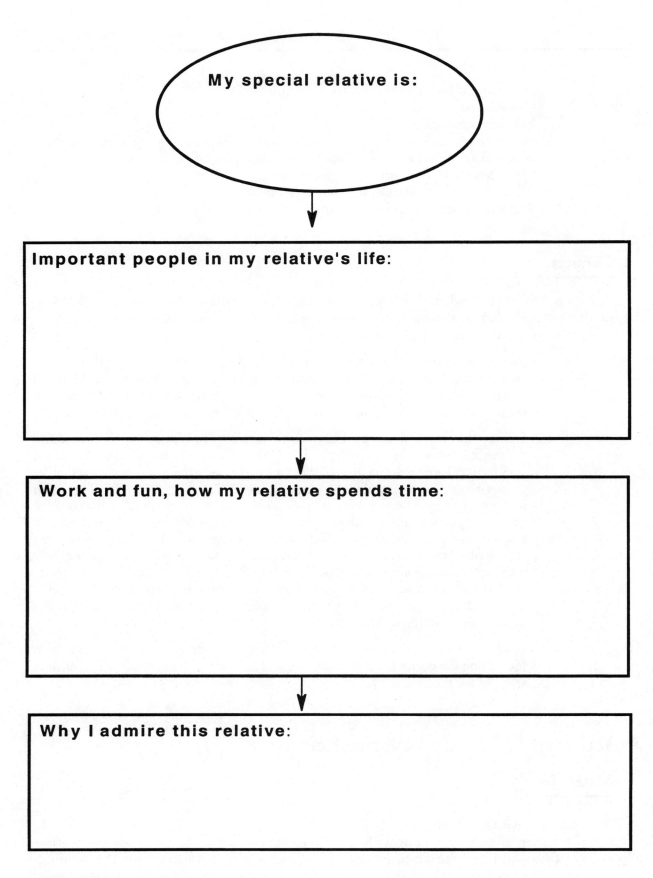

My special relative is:

Important people in my relative's life:

Work and fun, how my relative spends time:

Why I admire this relative:

➤Activity Sheet 4.1. Interview Web

My Bio-poem

Line 1: Write the first name of the special relative.

Line 2: List two traits that describe this relative.

Line 3: Write your name and describe your relationship to the special relative.

Relative of ...

Line 4: Describe activities, hobbies, jobs special to the relative.

Who likes ...

Line 5: Describe beliefs, attitudes, behaviors of the relative.

Who feels ...

Line 6: Add other information about the relative.

Who would like to see ...

Line 7: Tell where the relative lives.

Resident of ...

Line 8: Write the last name of the special relative.

➤ Activity Sheet 4.2. Bio-Poem Directions

Engage

Allen Say shared a special relationship with his grandfather. Ask students who the special relatives in their lives are.

Elaborate

To model using the interview web, ask for a student volunteer, then interview him or her and record the responses in the web (use activity sheet 4.1):

1. Who are the important people in the student's life? (Friend of, student of, son/daughter of, player of [list the coach's name]).

2. What activities are enjoyed by the student? What are accomplishments of the student? (Sports, awards, leisure time activities, vacation experiences, school subjects.)

3. Why is the student admired? (Invite positive comments from the class.)

Explore

Have students select family members with whom they share special relationships (aunts, uncles, cousins, grandparents) and complete interviewing webs (see activity sheet 4.1) to learn the information needed for the bio-poems. Review the interview information needs once again:

1. Important people in my relative's life: List people who are significant to the relative (e.g., daughter of, coach of, student of, proud parent of, friend of).

2. Work and fun: List all kinds of things the relative enjoys or has accomplished (e.g., sports, arts, awards, jobs, leisure time activities, vacation experiences).

3. Why I admire this relative: Write words and phrases that describe how you feel about the relative and why.

Give students several days to interview special relatives and gather their information.

Connect

Once interview information is gathered, have students follow the bio-poem format to write their poems (see activity sheet 4.2). Display the poem the students wrote about Grandfather and review activity sheet 4.2.

Following is a bio-poem, written about another favorite relative. It may also be helpful to students.

> Sarah
> Adventurous, glamorous
> Relative of Sarah James, her niece, who loves sharing her name.
> Who likes theater and dance, biography and mystery,

Who feels strongly about the environment, devoting her days to work at the nature center,
Who would like to see the jagged peaks of Nepal or grassy plains of Africa,
Resident of the snowy land of northern Minnesota and the sunny deserts of Arizona.
Manning

Circulate as students work on their poems and encourage them to discuss their ideas with peers as they develop the poems. When bio-poems are complete, have students print or type final copies. Use the final copies for the memory boxes lesson in Plan 3.

➤ Activity Plan 3: Creating Memory Boxes

Materials

Bio-poems students have completed about their relatives
Small pizza boxes, one per student (A local pizza company usually will donate the boxes.)
Tempera or poster paint (available at art stores or through the art teacher)
Sponge brushes (available at art stores or through the art teacher)
White glue thinned with water

Engage

Begin with this "quick think" activity: Have students draw large circles on sheets of paper, then within the circles draw symbols that represent their skills or accomplishments. Refocus question: What are accomplishments that make you feel proud? (A "quick think" is an open-ended puzzle for the brain or a wake-up call. Students will usually ask lots of questions about the "quick think" assignment; try not to elaborate or give more detailed instructions. Quietly repeat the original directions and encourage students to think deeply about what they have heard and make their own decisions. Some symbols they may come up with are footballs, baseballs, or other sporting equipment; chess pieces or other game symbols; ballet shoes; gymnastics equipment; books; and musical instruments.)

Elaborate

Open one of the pizza boxes and ask students: If you were creating memory boxes about yourselves, what objects, pictures, and things would you place in the boxes? (Favorite toy from childhood, a trophy, a souvenir from a special vacation journey, pictures of family, pets, and friends.)

Explore

Have students create memory boxes about the special relatives they wrote about in their bio-poems, following these instructions (this will take some time):

1. Use sponge brushes to paint the pizza boxes and let them dry overnight.

2. Plan the outside decorations: maps, drawings, photographs, small artifacts that are special to the relative. Use a mixture of white glue thinned with water as an adhesive, dip the sponge brushes in the adhesive, and attach the outside decorations. (Allow several days so students can devote lots of energy to planning and gathering materials.)

3. Frame or mount the bio-poem and paste it on the inside cover.

4. Plan the inside of the box so it is filled with pictures, mementos, and artifacts special to the relative. (Again, allow several days so students can give lots of energy to planning and gathering materials.)

Connect

Display the memory boxes and encourage students to share one or two favorite pieces from their boxes (e.g., a bio-poem and the significance of an object in the box, or maybe the significance of two objects in the box).

5 Hey, Al

Written by Arthur Yorinks
Illustrated by Richard Egielski
New York: Farrar, Straus & Giroux, 1986

Summary

➤ Al and his faithful dog, Eddie, are tired of life in the city: their apartment, the routine of their life, and the struggle to survive. When a parrot invites them to an island paradise they eagerly consent to the journey, and as the days pass blissfully and memories of their old life begin to fade, Al and Eddie decide that this island living is ecstasy; until the morning they awake to find they are turning into birds, with little beady eyes, beak-like noses, sprouting wings, and plumed tail feathers. Their dramatic escape and return to their former life in the city leads to them to the conclusion that there is no place like home.

Award Year

➤ 1987

Art Information

➤ Illustrated using watercolors.

Curriculum Connections

➤ Islands, with emphasis on the five themes of geography: location, place, human interaction, movement, and regions

➤ Activity Plan 1: Exploring Place and Sharing the Story

Materials

Music: "This Land Is Your Land" by Woody Guthrie and Arlo Guthrie, 1997.
(Available from Rounder Records, 1 Camp St., Cambridge, MA 02140,
800-768-6337; cost: about $15.00)
Caldecott Award poster
Watercolor paints (available at art stores)

Engage

Play "This Land Is Your Land" and introduce the theme of place: the physical and human characteristics that make a place special or unique. Have students look around the room and identify characteristics that make the room special or unique.

Elaborate

Introduce the story and have students think about the theme of place as they listen to the story. What do Al and Eddie realize about their home? How is it special or unique?

Explore

Have students compare the two places and make lists of what is special about each place (see figure 5.1). Ask them: How did Al and Eddie decide that there really is no place like home? (*Logical/Mathematical Intelligence*)

➤ Figure 5.1. City Home, Island Home

City Home	Island Home
One room on the West Side	Beautiful landscape: lush trees, rolling hills, gorgeous grass, and waterfalls.
They have each other, working, eating, and living together.	Birds of all kinds wait on them.
They get to be themselves, not turned into birds.	They eat, drink, swim, and sunbathe all day long.

Connect

Share the Caldecott Award information:

1. As students examine the cover of the book, ask them what special thing they notice. (gold medal) Ask them what the name of the medal is. (Caldecott Award Medal) Ask them why it has been placed on this book. (Some responses may be that the illustrations are special, well done, particularly interesting, exciting, and/or unusual.)

2. Discuss the art techniques used in creating the pictures. Richard Egielski uses strong color contrasts to reinforce the differences between Al's city home and the island paradise; muted browns and grays color the city home, and a bold palette of primary colors illustrates the island paradise. Have students browse the pictures to notice the color contrasts. Then look at the final illustration of the story, where Al brings the tropical colors to his city home.

   Two other illustrations that are fun to linger over are the flight to the island and the double-page illustration of the birds of the island paradise. Ask students to find the face in the island in the first picture. Ask them what connections come to mind as they look at the shape of the face. (a camel, another unusual bird) As students look at the birds in the second picture, ask them which birds they would choose to be. Be sure they give reasons for their choices.

3. Ask two student volunteers to search the poster for the year the story won. (Searching the poster helps students become familiar with the many different titles selected for the award.)

➤ Activity Plan 2: Exploring Location

Materials

Globes or desk maps showing longitude and latitude
Geography journals (spiral notebooks)

Engage

Write these two phrases on the board: "absolute location," "relative location." Ask the students what they mean. (Absolute location identifies a location's position on the globe, using longitude and latitude coordinates, or other absolute identifying points, like a post office mailing address; relative location describes where the place is located in relation to another place on Earth.)

Talk to the students about the following examples:

1. Our school: What is the absolute location of our school? (postal address of the school) How would you tell the relative location of our school? (two blocks east of Wal-Mart, across the street from the public library, etc.)

2. Your home: What is the absolute location of your home? (Have students work with partners to describe the relative locations of their homes.)

Elaborate

Ask students if they know how geographers describe absolute location. (with coordinates of longitude and latitude) Review the concepts of longitude and latitude, and have students use geography journals to record the information.

Have students plot the following coordinates and identify the places:

42° N, 88° W: What city? (Chicago, Illinois)

0°, 90° W: What islands? (Galapagos Islands)

30° N, 120° E: What city? (Shanghai, China)

30° S, 28° E: What country? (South Africa)

43° N, 31° E: What sea? (Black Sea)

Explore

Have students work with partners to create longitude and latitude puzzles for the class. Each partnership should pick a place on Earth and provide these pieces of information about that place: absolute location (longitude/latitude), relative location, and one cultural or climatic clue. (*Logical/Mathematical Intelligence*)

Connect

Post the longitude/latitude puzzles and have students try to solve them. Discuss why it is important to have the ability to identify absolute locations, using the following narration:

I think about pioneer days. A pioneer family has traveled for miles and miles and finally settled on a plot of land in Kansas. How will they stake their claim so that no one else claims the land? How will they register their claim? Unless the land has been officially surveyed, their location descriptions have to do with rivers, hills, lakes, and valleys, and trees.

➤ Activity Plan 3: Exploring Regions

Materials

Globes (one per student partnership)

Engage

Spin the globe and ask students this question: How might geographers divide the world into regions? Have students use the globes to identify these regions: cold and hot regions, northern and southern hemispheres,, types of landscapes (desert regions, jungle regions, mountain regions), regions of the United States (Northeast, South, Midwest, Southwest, Pacific Coast, Rocky Mountain). (*Bodily/Kinesthetic Intelligence*)

Elaborate

Create a two-column chart. In the first column list the regions that the students brainstormed and in the second column list similar characteristics that make each area a region (see figure 5.2). For example, an area of land becomes part of the desert region if it has minimal rainfall, lots of sunshine, high temperatures, and an arid landscape.

Region	Characteristics
desert	lots of sun hot temperatures very little rain
Northeast region of the United States	big cities lots of industry

➤ Figure 5.2. Regions

Explore

Ask the students: If you were Al and Eddie and could move to any of these regions, where would you choose to live and why? Have students work with partners to brainstorm and discuss their ideas, then share their responses. (*Verbal/Linguistic and Interpersonal Intelligences*)

Connect

Ask the students to identify their favorite region, and why it is their favorite. Have them identify other popular regions, and why they are popular. (*Logical/Mathematical Intelligence*)

➤ Activity Plan 4: Exploring Movement

Engage

Run into the room, pick up the phone or access the computer e-mail, then explain to the students that movement (the fourth theme of geography) is not just about physically moving from one place to another, it also describes moving ideas and information.

Elaborate

Ask the students to identify ways to get from one place to another.

Explore

Divide the class into two groups and have students brainstorm all the ways to physically change locations (transportation) and all the ways to communicate across the world. (*Interpersonal Intelligence*)

Connect

Have students use charades to share the results of their brainstorming. (*Bodily/Kinesthetic Intelligence*)

➤ Activity Plan 5: Exploring Human Interaction

Materials

Drawing paper (one sheet per student partnership)
Illustrating materials (crayons, colored pencils, markers)

Engage

Ask students to look around the room and then draw an example of one way in which they and you have individualized the room (examples: decorations, furniture, machinery, curtains, plants, name tags on desks). (*Visual/Spatial Intelligence*)

Elaborate

Address the students as follows:

What are ways in which we change the environment? Human interaction, our next theme of geography, talks about how we use the resources of the natural setting to live more effectively. Think about our community and how it is organized and structured. What are changes we've made? [Bridges, electrical lines, sewer systems, water and gas systems, housing additions, schools, businesses, parks, swimming pools, restaurants, roads, and dams are some examples.]

Explore

Ask the students to identify resources of their environment and how society is using them? (forests, rivers, minerals, land) Have students work with partners to illustrate examples of resources and their uses. They should fold a piece of paper in half; draw the resource in the first half; then draw how it is used in their community in the second half (see figure 5.3 for some ideas that could be illustrated). (*Visual/Spatial Intelligence*)

➤ **Figure 5.3. Resources in the Environment**

A Resource from Our Community	How We Use It
open land	farming
trees	lumber, shade, beauty
river	movement of goods, fishing

➤ Activity Plan 6: Creating an Island

Materials

Large sheets of butcher paper for each group (Map makers and locators will create map landscapes on the butcher paper sheets and the islands created by the geographers will be placed on these backdrops.)

Multiple copies of the "Imaginary Islands: Roles for the Project" (figure 5.4; one per student; individual copies will help the students be clear about the responsibilities of each role.)

Figure 5.5, Checklist of Requirements (one per student; individual copies will help the students support and encourage each other and independently check their progress in completing all the requirements for the island project.)

Engage

Write the five themes of geography on the board: location, place, movement, human interaction, and region.

Elaborate

Ask students to define or describe the purpose or subject of each theme. Review what each theme describes:

1. *Location* tells geographers where the place is. Location can be written in longitude and latitude terms, post office address terms, and relative or descriptive terms.

2. *Place* tells geographers the special features of a location: the land forms and water-ways, the plant and animal life, the natural resources, and the people who live there.

3. *Movement* describes transportation, trade, and communication or how people travel and talk with one another and how goods and services are shared or traded.

4. *Human interaction* looks at humans and the places where they live and describes the changes that happen because of the people living there.

5. *Regions* are areas into which geographers group parts of the world with similar characteristics or features.

The Locator

Your jobs are to select the absolute location of the new island, to describe the relative location of the island, and to assist the mapmaker.

Think about these questions: What is your hemisphere region? What are the longitude and latitude coordinates of the island? In what ocean, sea, or other body of water is the island located? How would you describe the location of the island in relative terms?

The Geographer

Your goals are to identify the physical characteristics of the island (land, water, and vegetation), determine what inhabitants the island has, and build the island terrain.

Think about these questions: What are the major physical features of the island? What places of interest might attract tourists? Who lives on the island?

The Traveler

You determine the primary transportation and communication methods for the island and build models to show how they function.

Think about these questions: How do the inhabitants travel and how are products moved on the island? How do the inhabitants communicate with each other and how does the island communicate with other places in the region?

►Figure 5.4. Imaginary Islands: Roles for the Project

The Environmentalist

You have two tasks: to design and build a model shelter for the inhabitants and to determine the economy of the island.

Think about these questions: How do the inhabitants use the land on the island? How do the inhabitants earn a living? What jobs are available to the inhabitants? How have the inhabitants changed the environment? What kind of homes do the inhabitants build?

The Mapmaker

Work with the locator and develop a climate report for the island. Also create a large detailed map showing the region of the world in which the island is located.

Think about these questions: What seasons happen on the island? What kind of weather happens on the island?

➤ Figure 5.4. Imaginary Islands: Roles for the Project (*cont.*)

Explore

Introduce the islands project with the following narration:

The five themes of geography that we have been studying can be our organizing tool for designing and creating new lands like the island in the sky Eddie and Al visited. You will be working in groups and your job will be designing and building original islands. Each one of you will have a special role in your group, so the group is counting on your enthusiastic and thorough participation. Let's look at the roles; as you hear the descriptions and the responsibilities, be thinking about the role you will choose. [Have students read along using Figure 5.4.]

Checklist of Requirements

Locator	Figured out the absolute location.	Helped the mapmaker.	Prepared a talk that describes the relative location of the island.
Geographer	Built the island terrain (land, water, vegetation).	Built at least one model of the inhabitants.	Prepared a talk that describes the island and its inhabitants.
Traveler	Built a transportation model.	Built communication model.	Prepared a talk that describes trade and communication.
Environmentalist	Built a shelter for the inhabitants.	Showed the jobs of the island.	Prepared a talk that describes the economy of the island.
Mapmaker	Prepared a large detailed map as a backdrop for the island.	Worked with the locator.	Prepared a climate report telling about the seasons and weather of the island.

▶ Figure 5.5. Checklist of Requirements

The *locator's* jobs are to select the absolute location of the new island, describe the relative location of the island, and assist the mapmaker. Think about how the locator would answer these questions: What is the hemisphere region? What are the longitude and latitude coordinates of the island? In what ocean, sea, or other body of water is the island located? How would the locator describe the location of the island in relative terms?

The *geographer's* goals are to identify the physical characteristics of the island (land, water, and vegetation), determine what inhabitants the island has, and build the island terrain. The geographer should think about how to answer these questions: What are the major physical features of the island? What places of interest might attract tourists? Who lives on the island? Think about the inhabitants of the island in *Hey, Al* and imagine who the inhabitants might be. Remember, they do not have to be people. How will the geographer show the inhabitants?

The *traveler* determines the primary transportation and communication methods for the island and builds models to show how they function. The traveler has to answer these questions: How do the inhabitants travel and how are products moved on the island? How do the inhabitants communicate with each other and how does the island communicate with other places in the region?

The *environmentalist* has two tasks: to design and build a model shelter for the inhabitants and to determine the economy or the ways in which the inhabitants earn a living on the island. The environmentalist tries to answer these questions: How do the inhabitants use the land on the island? How do the inhabitants earn a living? What jobs are available to the inhabitants? How have the inhabitants changed the environment? What kinds of homes do the inhabitants build?

The *mapmaker* works with the locator to develop a climate report for the island; these two also create a large, detailed map showing the region of the world in which the island is located and the longitude and latitude lines. The mapmaker will answer these questions: What seasons happen on the island? What kinds of weather happen on the island?

Divide students into small groups; have the groups meet and divide the role responsibilities. Each group will have someone in each role. As a first task for each group, the locator needs to decide the hemisphere region and the absolute location, because this location will affect the work of the other students in the group. For example, if the locator chooses a northern hemisphere location in the Arctic ocean, the geographer, the traveler, the environmentalist, and the mapmaker will need to consider how the snow and ice in this location will affect the terrain and the vegetation, the inhabitants and their shelters and jobs, the trade and communication, and the seasons and the weather. Circulate as students work, to monitor progress and judge how much time will be needed for the project. Encourage students to refer to the checklist (figure 5.5).

Connect

Display the imaginary islands and have students share information about them.

6 Jumanji

Written by Chris Van Allsburg
Illustrated by Chris Van Allsburg
Boston: Houghton Mifflin, 1981

Summary

➤ Judy and Peter find a game at the park and decide to play it. At home again, the children set up the game. Judy reads the directions and Peter goes first, not really expecting the game to be exciting. He rolls a seven, moves to that square, and reads the message, "lion attacks, move back two spaces." As he prepares to move back two spaces Judy whispers a warning and Peter turns to see a lion lying on the piano licking his lips. Subsequent moves bring more dangers—monkeys, monsoons, a herd of rhinos, a python—until Judy rolls a six and arrives at the golden city of Jumanji and magically everything returns to normal. The adventure continues when they return the game to the park and it's taken by the Budwing boys, who never read directions.

Award Year

➤ 1982

Art Information

➤ Illustrated using Conté dust and Conté pencil.

Curriculum Connections

➤ Biomes of the world

➤Activity Plan 1: Sharing the Story

Materials

Game box (covered with paper and labeled *Jumanji*)

Dice

Game sheet (Transfer the game board shape to a large [double-bed size] sheet and color with permanent markers; see figure 6.1.)

Caldecott Award poster

Conté chalks (available at art stores in black, white, sanguine, and sepia)

Cotton balls

Paper plates (two or three per student; buy inexpensive paper plates, the kind that come 50 or 100 to a package.)

Three or four thesaurus dictionaries

Opera tape (Check the library for recordings of these operas: *Hansel and Gretel* and *Amahl and the Night Visitors.*)

Listening station (recorder and earphones)

Drawing paper (one sheet per student)

Illustrating materials (crayons, colored pencils, markers)

Preplanning with the librarian (During discovery center time, student partnerships will be visiting the library to check out other stories by Van Allsburg; ask the librarian to reserve these titles.)

Engage

Examine the cover and talk about the title. Ask students: With a title like this, what do you think the story will be? From the title, *Jumanji*, what will be the location of the story? Show the game box, roll the dice, and ask students to speculate how they are connected to the story. (*Verbal/ Linguistic Intelligence*)

Elaborate

Be as dramatic as possible when you share the story.

Explore

Heave a big sigh, sit back, and digest the story for a moment. Ask the students: What is one adjective you would use to describe the story? Why? How is this a fantasy? What will be the consequences for Daniel and Walter, who never read instructions when they play games? Display the sheet showing the enlarged game board and explain that the class will have an opportunity to play the game once the research contributions are completed.

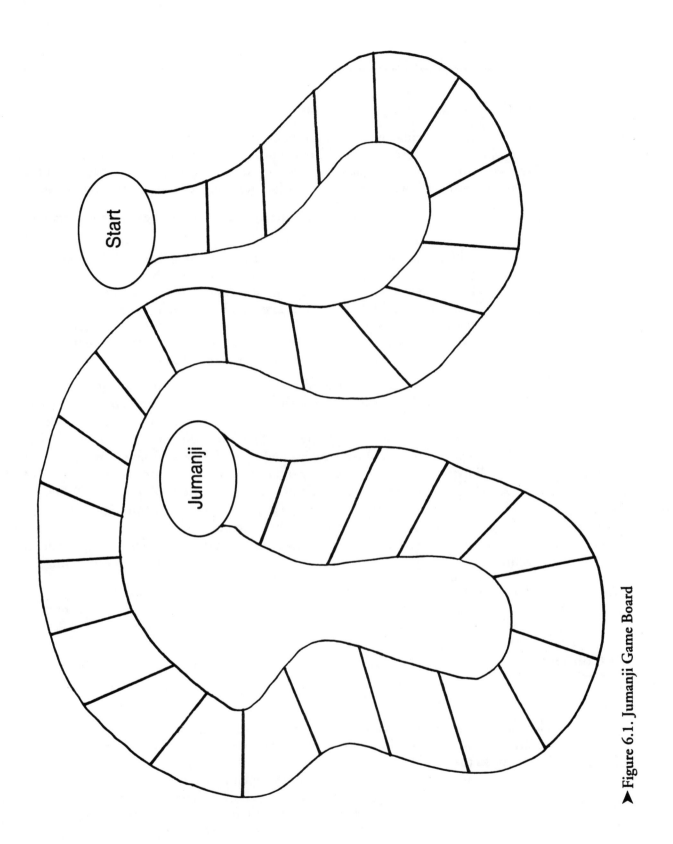

► Figure 6.1. Jumanji Game Board

Share the Caldecott Award information:

1. As students examine the cover of the book, ask them what special thing they notice. (gold medal) Ask them what the name of the medal is. (Caldecott Award Medal) Ask them why it has been placed on this book. (Some responses may be that the illustrations are special, well done, particularly interesting, exciting, and/or unusual.)

2. Discuss the art techniques used in creating the pictures using the following narration:

   > In his acceptance speech for the Caldecott Award, Mr. Van Allsburg said that some of the inspiration for the story came from a childhood fascination with seeing things in places where they normally do not belong (e.g., a newspaper clipping showing a car's front end sitting in a living room). We have lots of examples in this story: the lion on the piano, monkeys on the kitchen table, rain indoors, the guide who is lost, rhinos charging through the living room, the tsetse fly, the python on the mantel, and the erupting volcano.

   > The gray backgrounds in the illustrations come from ground Conté dust applied with a cotton ball and the white and dark figures are created using the whole Conté chalks. It's interesting to see how much variety and depth are present in the pictures through the blending of these light and dark chalks. The shifts in perspective are also interesting and move the reader from impartial observer (the illustrations of the trip to the park, the set up of the game, and the arrival of Daniel and Walter) to active participant in the emotions of the game. When we browse the pictures drawn from a low angle perspective, we are right there with Peter and Judy and feel their terror when the lion and the python appear, their dismay at the arrival of the monkeys, their despair at the rain and the charging rhinos, and their anxiety when the volcano erupts and the game seems never-ending.

3. Ask two student volunteers to search the poster for the year the story won. (Searching the poster helps students become familiar with the many different titles selected for the award.)

Connect

Introduce the discovery centers as follows:

There are four centers: art, music, vocabulary word banks, and reading. When we discussed the pictures in the story we learned that Van Allsburg used Conté chalks to create them. In the art center, you will have opportunities to draw your own pictures using the chalks. In the opening pages of *Jumanji*, we learned that Peter and Judy's parents were leaving for the opera. In the music center, you will have a chance to listen to an opera and imagine scenes from the story that is told through the music. Van Allsburg also had a wonderful way with words, so the vocabulary center is a time to look at the story again and continue building our word banks for writing. The reading center will be an opportunity to go to the library and find other stories written by Van Allsburg.

THE OPERA

Peter and Judy's parents went to the opera. Listen to the opera tape, imagine a scene from the story you are hearing, and draw a picture to accompany what you hear. Describe to the class what you thought was the story of the opera you heard. (*Musical/Rhythmic Intelligence*)

ILLUSTRATING

Look at the illustrations in the book, then use the Conté chalks to make your own drawing. Experiment with a cotton ball to see its effect on the chalk. (*Visual/Spatial Intelligence*)

READING

What are other stories written by Mr. Van Allsburg? Visit the library with a partner, use the library catalog to identify another story, find the book on the shelf, and check it out. Read the story and prepare an oral book review for the class. Don't reveal the ending when you and your partner tell about the story. (*Verbal/Linguistic Intelligence*)

Biome Research

Map: On a map of the world, use colored pencil to locate your biome. Be sure to create a map key. Paste your map in the center of your game board poster.

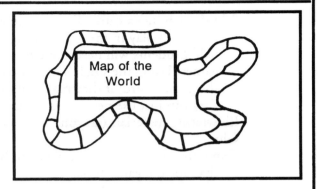

Gameboard: Draw the shape of your gameboard around the map.

The Land and Plant Life: If you were a scientist exploring this biome, what landforms and plant life would you see? Research and take notes on the land and plant life in the biome. Decorate your biome gameboard with a landscape scene that shows the biome at a glance (land and plants). Hint: One partner should research plants and one partner should research the land of the biome.

Animal Life: Research the animal life of the biome. What animals live there? What adaptations help them survive in this biome? Use your research notes to create instructions for the squares of your gameboard; be sure to write the instructions on the index cards, then paste these on your gameboard. For example, if you were the taiga, one game square might read "Moose migrate to feeding grounds, lose one turn;" another might say "Beavers fell trees and make bridge over icy river, move ahead five spaces." Other examples from the temperate forest include: "You become a black bear, winter arrives and you hibernate, move back four spaces;" "Deer tracks criss-cross the snow and provide an easy path for walking, move ahead three spaces."

Climate: Research the climate of the biome. Use the information to make more instructions for the squares of your gameboard. For example, if you were the desert biome, one square might read "Night brings cooling temperatures and a full moon, move ahead six spaces." A tundra square might say "Blizzard swirls, lose two turns."

➤Activity Sheet 6.1. Biome Research Sheet

3. The next step will be to research the land and plant life of the biome. Use this information to plan and color the background of your game board. You want it to look like a landscape painting.

4. Animal life and climate in your biome will provide the instructions for the game squares. Be sure the instructions fit the facts of your biome. For example, if you are studying the tundra (snow-covered lands in the far North) and one of your game squares reads "Monkeys surround and frighten you, move back two spaces," this would not fit the facts of the tundra because monkeys do not live in the tundra.

5. Here are the choices for researching the biomes: cool grasslands (prairies), hot grasslands (savannas), temperate forests (conifers), temperate forests (deciduous), tropical forests, tundra, taiga, deserts, mountains, chaparral, and oceans (see figure 6.3). (Place the choices in a basket and let students draw choices and begin their research.) (*Visual/Spatial, Verbal/Linguistic, and Interpersonal Intelligences*)

Connect

Display the biome game boards and have student partnerships present what they have learned about their biomes. Schedule a time to play the games; students may play the games they created or may trade and play another partnership's biome game. Use math tiles and dice for playing pieces. (*Bodily/Kinesthetic Intelligence*)

➤ Culminating Activity Plan

Materials

Jumanji game sheet, from introductory lesson (see figure 6.1)
3-by-5-inch index cards
Game tiles and dice

Playing the Game

Have students select two favorite instruction squares from their biome games, transfer the instructions to the reserved index cards, and attach student-created game squares to the game board sheet. Evenly distribute the student-created game cards in the squares of the board. Divide the class in half. Half of the class will roll the dice and move their game markers along the board. The other half of the class will dramatize the events on the board game as they happen. Switch rolls so everyone will have opportunities to play both positions.

cool grasslands (prairies)

hot grasslands (savannas)

temperate forests (conifers)

temperate forests (deciduous)

tropical forests

tundra

taiga

deserts

mountains

chaparral

oceans

➤ Figure 6.3. Biome Research Choices

7 The Little House

Written by Virginia Lee Burton
Illustrated by Virginia Lee Burton
Boston: Houghton Mifflin, 1942, 1969

Summary

➤ A little house experiences the seasons and the changes brought by development and expansion of a city. The setting on the hill is a wonderful place for the house, but slowly the far-distant city grows until it completely surrounds the little house. The house grows more and more unkempt and lonely until one day it is moved to a new place in the country, given a new coat of paint, and once again the house is happy and enjoying the seasons of the year.

Award Year

➤ 1943

Art Information

➤ Illustrated using watercolors.

Curriculum Connections

➤ Communities

➤ Activity Plan 1: Sharing the Story

Materials

> Drawing paper (one sheet per student)
> Mural paper (Tear a long sheet of butcher paper and divide it into twelve 24 inch
>   sections. See figure 7.1.)
> Illustrating materials (crayons, markers, paints, or colored pencils)
> Caldecott Award poster
> Watercolor paints (available at art stores)
> Paintbrush

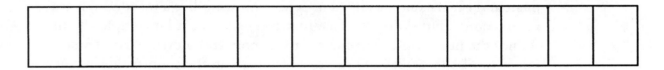

24-by-24 inch squares

➤ **Figure 7.1. Mural Diagram**

Engage

Start with this "quick think" activity: Have students draw rectangles, and in one minute of time, use a variety of lines (straight, curved, diagonal, irregular) to change the rectangles to represent a new idea. The goal of a quick think is to awaken the brain and have students begin to think in open-ended ways. Students often ask clarification questions about the size of the rectangle or its placement on the page; try not to elaborate and give additional directions, just repeat the first direction and encourage them to imagine what they could do. Collect the drawings and comment on the changes made to the rectangles. Some changes you may see are houses, gift boxes, fences, books, framed photographs or pictures, or doghouses. (*Visual/Spatial Intelligence*)

Elaborate

Introduce the story and have students note all the changes experienced by the house as you share the story.

Explore

Brainstorm a list of the changes that happened to the little house (springtime, summer days, fall, winter, the road widens, houses surround the little house, apartments and stores, streetlights, the arrival of the trolley line, the elevated train is added and then the subway comes, skyscrapers, and return to the country and a new look). Divide a long piece of paper into twelve sections and have students work in partnerships to illustrate the stages of the little house. (*Visual/Spatial and Interpersonal Intelligences*)

As a homework assignment, ask students to walk in their neighborhoods and notice the variety in living places. Students should select one living place and draw a picture of it; encourage them to be careful with details and encourage variety: apartment house, mobile homes, two-story, one-story, brick, stone, wood, modern, old-fashioned, and split level. Display drawings and conduct several discussion sessions comparing and contrasting similarities and differences. (*Visual/Spatial Intelligence*)

Connect

Share the Caldecott Award information:

1. As students examine the cover of the book, ask them what special thing they notice? (gold medal) Ask them what the name of the medal is. (Caldecott Award Medal) Ask them why it has been placed on this book. (Some responses may be that the illustrations are special, well done, particularly interesting, exciting, and/or unusual.)

2. Discuss the art techniques used in creating the pictures. Ask the students these questions: When was the little house the happiest? The saddest? When had it experienced the biggest change? How does the illustrator help us see these changes? (Browse the pictures and notice the increasing use of brown, gray, and black in the watercolor illustrations.) Talk to the students about the changes in color as follows:

   > The colors in the opening illustrations of the passing seasons have a feeling of happiness and lightness, reinforcing how much the house enjoys its perch on the hillside in the country. The softness of the colors and the openness of the space begin to change on page 14 and our eyes are drawn to the trucks, the road, and the exhaust from the steam shovel. The dark colors of the growing city begin to overpower the house until, on page 31, the house is hardly noticed in the bright lights of the city windows. Then, as the house is moved back to the country, the colors soften and return us to the sense of happiness and space.

   > A recurring figure used in Burton's illustrations is what she calls the "swing tree," and it's here in *The Little House*. (Point out the tree in the opening illustrations to the right of the house, then have students continue browsing to notice its disappearance as modernization begins to surround the house.) The "swing tree" reappears to the left of the house in the final illustration; its presence at the end seems to indicate a return to the happy, fun time of the beginning of the story.

Another comment often made by students focuses on the placement of the windows, door, and porch and how much this arrangement resembles a face and personalizes the fate of the house. The curve of the porch seems to move from smiling mouth to downturned mouth, surrounded by noise and confusion, back to smiling mouth when once again the house sits on a new foundation in the country.

3. Ask two student volunteers to search the poster for the year the story won. (Searching the poster helps students become familiar with the many different titles selected for the award.)

➤Activity Plan 2: Designing Living Spaces

Materials

Guest speaker: architect (To find an architect, use the yellow pages of the phone book, make a phone call to the Chamber of Commerce, or review student information sheets for occupations of parents.)

What It Feels Like to Be a Building by Forrest Wilson (The Preservation Press, National Trust for Historic Preservation, 1785 Massachusetts Ave., N.W., Washington, DC 20036)

Engage

What It Feels Like to Be a Building has some great opportunities for body movements; share the book and dramatize the body movements whenever possible:

- *Columns*: stand tall and sometimes bend when they are thin

- *Beams*: push together, pull apart, and butt heads

- *Corbels*: droop and hold a weight on your back

- *Arches*: three students squeeze and push

- *Buttresses*: support a person

Elaborate

Have the architect explain to the students the process for designing and building living spaces.

Explore

Have students think and work as architects, select a client, and build a living space to meet the client's needs. One of your jobs will be to role play the needs of a client if students do not understand how to proceed; have them meet with you as an architect would, ask questions, and receive clarification on your needs. The descriptions of the clients are intentionally brief so that students will be encouraged to thoughtfully analyze the information to identify the consequences of these needs (e.g., what kind of house is needed for a family of eight who also have dogs and cats that they love? Will each child have a bedroom? Will the animals be outdoor animals? Where will they live?).

Connect

Present the finished structures to the class; in the presentations, have students identify specifically how they met the needs of the clients. (*Logical/Mathematical, Visual/Spatial, Bodily/Kinesthetic, Verbal/Linguistic Intelligences*)

Clients

- The Westons are a large family of eight. They love and have pets, two dogs and two cats.

- The Burkes have grown tired of commuting to the city on a daily basis. They want a carefree home in the city where they can life comfortably during the week.

- The Andersons are tired of high utility bills and want to investigate solar energy or wind energy. They live in Tucson, Arizona.

- The Edwards work from home.

- The Buntings are moving to a mountaintop home in Colorado. They have lots of junk that they can't throw away.

➤Activity Plan 3: What Is a Community?

Materials

Three circles made from paper, in graduated sizes (See figure 7.2; students will be adding information and pictures to each circle, so be sure the village circle is large enough to hold some additional writing and artwork.)

Three additional paper circles in graduated sizes (See figure 7.3; students will also be adding information and pictures to each of these circles, so be sure the urban circle is large enough to hold some additional writing and artwork.)

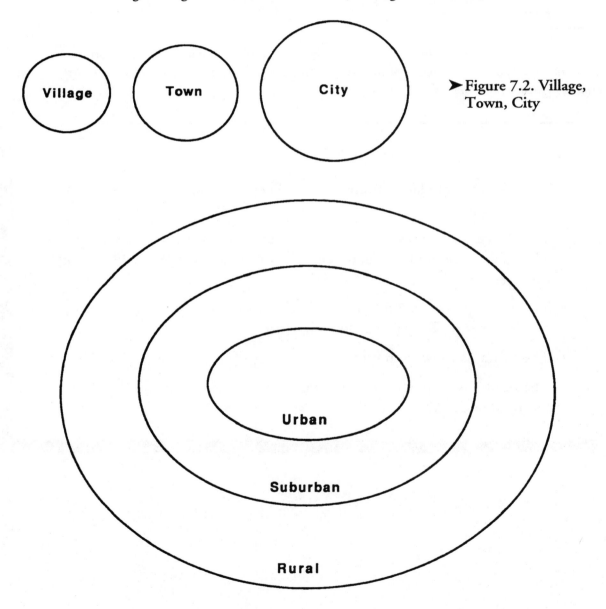

➤Figure 7.2. Village, Town, City

➤Figure 7.3. Urban, Suburban, Rural

Engage

Use the circles to create two bulletin board displays, then point to the circles and ask students if they can describe the differences between these terms. This is a thinking question, so don't worry if the information is inaccurate.

Elaborate

Divide students into six groups: city, town, village, suburb, rural, and urban. Have them use dictionaries and encyclopedias to gather information about each term, then brainstorm and create ways to show the information in picture form. See figure 7.4 if students are stumped for ideas. (*Verbal/Linguistic, Visual/Spatial, and Interpersonal Intelligences*)

Defining the Terms	
City	<u>land use</u>: not much open space: pictures showing many streets <u>business</u>: pictures of lots of businesses <u>housing</u>: pictures of places to live: row houses, apartments, lofts <u>people</u>: pictures of crowds <u>transportation</u>: pictures of subways, buses, elevated trains, trolleys
Town	<u>land use</u>: more open space: pictures showing some streets <u>business</u>: pictures of local businesses <u>housing</u>: pictures of houses, some apartments <u>people</u>: pictures of people but not crowds <u>transportation</u>: pictures of cars, bicycles
Village	<u>land use</u>: lots of open space: picture showing a main street and maybe one or two side streets <u>business</u>: pictures of a post office, maybe a country store. <u>housing</u>: pictures of a few houses <u>people</u>: pictures of a few people <u>transportation</u>: pictures showing walking, bicycles, a few cars
Rural	pictures of farms and ranches
Suburban	pictures of neighborhoods
Urban	pictures of skyscrapers

➤ Figure 7.4. Defining the Terms

Explore

Discuss the results of the students' research. Ask them these questions: What similarities do you see among these places? (people, work, living) What are the key differences? (size, space, structures) How is each a community? (They are all places where people live and work.)

Connect

Ask students to define the "community." (A place where people live and work together; sometimes they share common interests.) Ask them these questions: Is a school a community? (Yes, because during the day we live and work together.) What are other examples of communities? (business, church, sports team)

➤ Activity Plan 4: Location Makes All the Difference

Materials

Drawing paper (one sheet per student)
Illustrating materials (markers, crayons, colored pencils)
Bulletin board space or a long sheet of paper (to construct the timeline)

Engage

Ask students: If you were going to create a new community, where would you locate it and why?

Elaborate

Ask students these questions about their own community: What location advantages drew settlers to our community? Why did the community develop? What is its history? What history is being made now?

Explore

Create a visual timeline of the history of the community that students described above (see figure 7.5). Use local resources, such as guest speakers, newspaper archives, books, and historical society materials, to explore the history of the community. If students and their families have lived in the community for a long time, encourage students to discuss the project with their families. (*Verbal/ Linguistic and Logical/Mathematical Intelligences*)

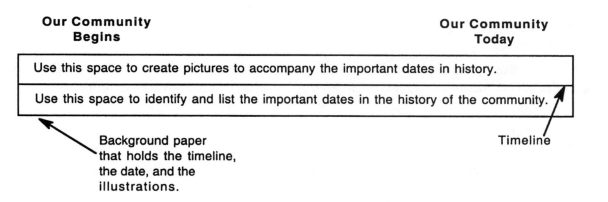

➤ Figure 7.5. The History of Our Community

Connect

Tour the timeline and have students share one or two highlights from their events.

➤ Activity Plan 5: Growing and Surviving

Materials

Telephone books (one per small group)
Field trip planning (Plan a walking tour of the community.)
Field trip recording supplies (sketch pads, cameras, tape recorders, notebooks)
Materials for students to decorate a bulletin board (paper, markers, etc.)

Engage

Ask the students to identify the necessary resources that help a community grow and survive. (health care, government, recreation, transportation, housing, food and water, clothing, safety, home maintenance and furnishing, and education are some examples; for more ideas, have students browse the yellow pages of the phone book to develop categories of resources, rather than individual businesses.)

Elaborate

Ask students for examples of these resources in their community. Refocus question: What places illustrate or explain examples of these resources in our community? Brainstorm and choose one to locate on the field trip. (Students may take sketch pads, cameras, tape recorders, notebooks, etc., on the field trip to record images.)

Explore

Plan a field trip into the community and have students use a variety of tools to write about, draw, take pictures of, and record the resources they locate in the community.

Connect

When students return, those who chose the same category of resource will work together and create a display for the bulletin board. After bulletin board displays are created and shared, have students reflect on this question in their journals: What do you think are the most important resources for a community? (*Verbal/Linguistic, Visual/Spatial, Bodily/Kinesthetic, Interpersonal, and Intrapersonal Intelligences*)

➤ Activity Plan 6: Goods and Services

Materials

Field trip planning (Plan a visit to an important business in the community.)
Business products (Gather a variety of items produced by businesses in the community and create a display of the products. For example, a can of oil from a local oil company, tissue products from a major paper products manufacturer, envelopes from an envelope manufacturer, several antiques, and a light bulb for the work of a power plant.)

Engage

Display the business products and discuss why they are important to the community (jobs, money, support for education and government, useful products).

Elaborate

Take a field trip to an important business in the community.

Explore

In the follow-up discussion, talk about these terms—*goods, services, income, assembly line, product, manufacturing, industry, trade*—in connection with the business you visited. Ask the students questions such as: What goods were sold by the company we visited? What services did they need to produce the goods? What is their source of income? How did production work? How did the company advertise its product?

Connect

Sponsor a business fair. Brainstorm a list of goods and services needed in the school community and have students work in small groups to create booths that advertise and sell those goods and services. Some examples are post office services (so students can mail school pen pal letters), library services (older students can help younger students choose new books for independent reading or assist with research), school supplies, and treats (e.g., ice cream or frozen fruit Popsicles). (*Verbal/Linguistic, Visual/Spatial, Bodily/Kinesthetic, and Interpersonal Intelligences*)

➤ Activity Plan 7: I Am a Citizen

Materials

Activity sheet 7.1, Job Application Sheet (multiple copies)

Engage

Begin a discussion on citizenship and have students identify characteristics of good citizens. Some responses may be: follows rules/laws; shows pride in best effort; demonstrates respect for authority, property, and others; has a positive attitude; helps others (friend or not); shows integrity (doing the right thing even when no one is watching); demonstrates responsibility (homework, organization, accountability).

Elaborate

Share some of the ways students will work as citizens during the year:

- *Class jobs*: Each quarter students will have opportunities to apply for class jobs. (*Bodily/Kinesthetic and Intrapersonal Intelligences*)

- *Examples of citizenship*: Students, parents, and you will keep a chart recording and acknowledging examples of citizenship throughout the year. (*Logical/Mathematical and Intrapersonal Intelligences*)

- *Serving the community*: Students will work in small groups to design and implement a service project in the school community and/or in the local community. (*Bodily/Kinesthetic and Interpersonal Intelligences*)

Explore

Brainstorm a list of class jobs and describe the responsibilities and the skills they require. Use activity sheet 7.1 to have students apply for the jobs they wish to hold. Review the applications and assign jobs.

Connect

Announce the class jobs and have students begin carrying out their responsibilities.

Name:
The job I wish to hold is:
I would be good at this job because:
Reference:

➤Activity Sheet 7.1. Job Application Sheet

8 *May I Bring a Friend?*

Written by Beatrice Schenk de Regniers
Illustrated by Beni Montresor
New York: Atheneum, 1982

Summary

➤ A young boy is invited by the King and Queen, not only to tea but also to breakfast, lunch, dinner, apple pie, and Halloween, and of course he must bring friends. Some are not the most well-behaved of animals, like hippo, who puts his foot in the cake and eats everything in sight, and the monkeys, who swing from the drapes and climb under the King's robe. Others have a problem with size, like giraffe, who is so large he almost covers the table, and elephant, who is so big he can't even sit at the table.

Award Year

➤ 1965

Art Information

➤ Illustrated using black line drawings alternated with color-washed two-page spreads.

Curriculum Connections

➤ Countries of the world: customs and traditions

➤ Activity Plan 1: Sharing the Story

Materials

> Caldecott Award poster
> Thin black marker
> Watercolor paints (available at art stores)
> Drawing paper (one sheet per student partnership)
> Illustrating materials (crayons, markers, colored pencils)
> Transparency of examples of new verses to continue the story (figure 8.1)

Engage

Ask the students: If you were invited to tea what would be appropriate behavior? How would you act on Apple Pie Day?

Explain to the students about different cultures using the following narration:

> Different countries have different customs. If you were in Barbados and folded your arms across your chest, you would be telling the person with whom you are speaking that you are giving them your complete attention. [Ask for two student volunteers and have them stand in front of the class facing each other, then have them move closer and closer to each other, until when they speak, they feel each other's breath.] Conversation space in many countries tends to be smaller than in the United States, where we are generally uncomfortable if someone moves that closely into our personal space, but in some countries like Argentina and countries of the Middle East it would be rude to stand far apart when conversing. [Have the students yawn.] In Colombia this is impolite and a sign of hunger. [Have students place hands under their elbows.] In Honduras, this means that someone is thought to be stingy.

Introduce the story and pose this question for students to think about as they listen: What advice would you give the guests in the story we are about to read?

Elaborate

Invite participation as you share the story by pausing to allow speculation by students on each page where the author has written, "So I brought my friend." Ask them who the friend might be.

The King and Queen invited me
on New Year's day for a sail at sea.

So I brought my friend ... (a reindeer)

My friend nibbled and chewed,
while we traveled the sea,
'til all that was left for me and the King,
was cider and a black-eyed pea.

The King and Queen
sent up a flare ...
"It's a Fourth of July display,
come watch and listen, if you dare!"

So I brought my friends ... (a flock of starlings)

My friends flittered and soared,
so loud was their chatter,
the boom of the cannon
did not even matter.

King and Queen scheduled
a joke-telling day ...
"Bring all of your favorites,
we'll tell jokes all through the day!"

So I brought my friend ... (a hyena)

My friend started with one,
then moved to center stage,
he laughed and laughed and told lots more,
King and Queen were soon in a rage.

➤ Figure 8.1. More Celebrations

The King and Queen
sent a balloon ...
"It's a birthday for the Queen,
we will celebrate at noon."

So I brought my friend ... (a polar bear)

My friend slurped up the green tea,
and gobbled shrimp from the dish.
He climbed on the walrus ice sculpture,
then granted the Queen her birthday wish.

The King and Queen said,
"Do come to our place
for a Valentine's Day party,
with plenty of candy and lace."

So I brought my friend ... (a new puppy)

My friend loved all the lace,
when I opened my gift,
my puppy got tangled in the ribbon,
soon looked like another Valentine's gift.

The King and Queen happily
dispatched a friendly invite ...
"It's a windy weekday,
so bring your top-notch kite!"

So I brought my friends ... (several garter snakes)

My friends were most excited,
they could hardly even wait,
to be tails on the kite,
was a wonderful fate.

➤ Figure 8.1. More Celebrations (*cont.*)

Explore

Ask the students: What problems do the guests in the story face? (Giraffe: elbows on the table; hippopotamus: feet in the cake; monkeys: all over the place; elephant: too big to sit; lions: roared too loudly; seal: no problem.) What would be your advice? Who would you invite? What difficulties might these guests face?

Share the Caldecott Award information:

1. As students examine the cover of the book, ask them what special thing they notice. (gold medal) Ask them what the name of the medal is. (Caldecott Award Medal) Ask them why it has been placed on this book. (Some responses may be that the illustrations are special, well done, particularly interesting, exciting, and/or unusual.)

2. Discuss the art techniques used in creating the pictures. Ask the students what pattern they notice in the illustrations. (Slowly browse the pages until students see the pattern: illustrations in pen and ink washed in one color, then pen and ink alone, then full color, but not really accurate full color, as students will notice when they look at the animals: a purple lion and a red hippopotamus.) Point out to students that it's an interesting effect, adding to the fun of the story. (Look again at the use of pen and ink to notice the detail: light and shadows, texture, shape.)

3. Ask two student volunteers to search the poster for the year the story won. (Searching the poster helps students become familiar with the many different titles selected for the award.)

Connect

The boy really enjoyed introducing his friends to the King and Queen and sharing these celebrations with them. Create a three-column chart on the board and label the columns: guests, celebrations, and potential problems. Ask students what animals they would invite, what the celebrations would be, and what the results might be. (See figure 8.2 for some examples.)

Some students may wish to use the ideas from the chart on the board to write their own verses; some may prefer just to illustrate already written verses (see figure 8.1 for examples of verses written from the ideas in figure 8.2). Have the students who are illustrating the already-written verses work with partners. They have the following five tasks to complete (be sure they use five pieces of drawing paper):

1. Type or print the first stanza (the invitation).

2. Type or print the words, "So I brought my friend . . . " (or friends).

3. Brainstorm and make a rough sketch of a picture showing the boy and the animal(s) arriving at the castle, then make a final picture.

4. Type or print the second stanza (the results).

5. Brainstorm and make a rough sketch of a picture showing how the animal acted at the celebration, then make a final picture.

Guests	Celebrations	Potential Problems
reindeer	New Year's day sail at sea	ate all the cider and black-eyed peas
polar bear	Queen's birthday	climbed on the ice sculpture
flock of starlings	Fourth of July celebration	chattered so loudly, they drowned out the boom of the cannon
a new puppy	Valentine's Day party	got tangled in the ribbon and lace
hyena	joke day	laughed and laughed and couldn't leave the stage
garter snakes	kite-flying day	the snakes became the tail of the kite

➤Figure 8.2. Guests for the Parties

Encourage the students who want to write their own verses to work with partners or in small groups because this will help add to the brainstorming possibilities. Have them follow the pattern in figure 8.1, instead of the four stanzas of the book. The first stanza should provide the invitation and name the event and the second stanza should tell what happens when the friend comes to the event. Lines two and four must rhyme, and the syllable count must be the same in lines one and two and lines three and four. The syllable count might be confusing for the students, but encourage them to think of lines one and two as a couplet (in terms of the number of syllables) and lines three and four as a new couplet that can have a different number of syllables. If students review the examples they will see that the syllable count is often different between the first couplet and the second couplet.

Use the second stanza of the garter snake rhyme to model an easy way to think of lots of rhyming words: If wait is the last word of line two, what words will rhyme with wait? Let's go down the letters of the alphabet; are there any "a" rhyming words, "b" rhyming words? (Encourage the students to play with the sounds; eventually their list will have these options: ate, bait, date, fate, gate, hate, Kate, late, mate, and rate.) This brainstorming strategy will give them lots of choices as they compose their stanzas.

Once the two stanzas are written, have one student prepare the three pages of writing (the stanza one page, the "So I brought my friend(s) . . . " page, and the stanza two page; see figure 8.3), and have the other students in the group brainstorm and prepare illustrations for the verses (the arrival picture and the behavior at the celebration picture).

Have students brainstorm a title for the book, create the title page, and assemble the book, using figure 8.3 as the pattern. (*Verbal/Linguistic, Interpersonal, and Visual/Spatial Intelligences*)

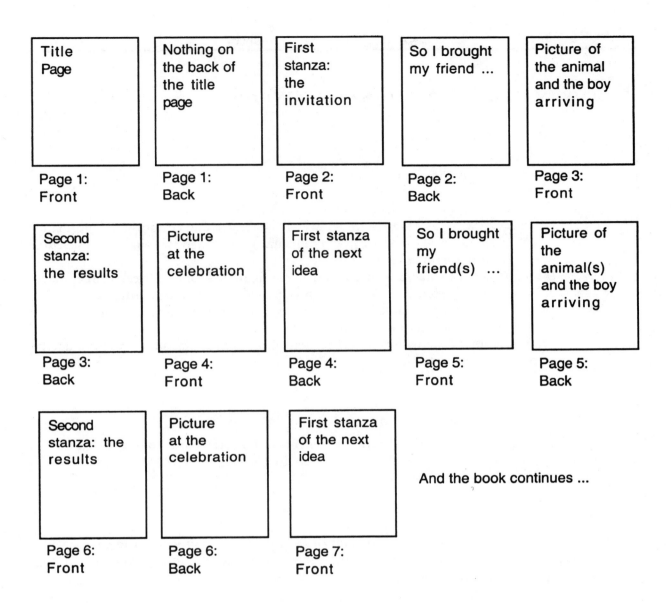

Title Page	Nothing on the back of the title page	First stanza: the invitation	So I brought my friend ...	Picture of the animal and the boy arriving
Page 1: Front	Page 1: Back	Page 2: Front	Page 2: Back	Page 3: Front
Second stanza: the results	Picture at the celebration	First stanza of the next idea	So I brought my friend(s) ...	Picture of the animal(s) and the boy arriving
Page 3: Back	Page 4: Front	Page 4: Back	Page 5: Front	Page 5: Back
Second stanza: the results	Picture at the celebration	First stanza of the next idea	And the book continues ...	
Page 6: Front	Page 6: Back	Page 7: Front		

➤ Figure 8.3. Layout of the Book

➤Activity Plan 2: Countries of the World

Materials

Research journals (spiral notebook)
World map
Colorful dot stickers (available at most office supply stores)
Preplanning with the librarian (Students will be researching customs and information about countries of the world, and preplanning helps identify sources and schedule times for researching.)
Multiple copies of the research assignments in figure 8.4 for each week (Either make enough copies so the assignments can be pasted into research journals or make just a few copies available in the classroom and the library that students can use if they need reminders about each assignment.)
Multiple copies of activity sheet 8.1 for recording country statistics (one per student or student partnership)

Engage

Display the world map and invite students to brainstorm about countries that interest them. Discuss what makes them curious about these countries.

Elaborate

Decide if students will work individually or with partners or if they can choose which way to work, then have students select the countries they will investigate. Place the colorful stickers on these countries and display the world map on a bulletin board in the classroom or in the hallway.

Explore

Briefly describe the assignments of the coming weeks, then focus on the assignment for the current week and explain this one in detail (see figure 8.4). Have students record the requirements of the assignment in their research journals so they will be clear about their tasks:

In our bodily/kinesthetic week we will focus on the sports, dances, and recreation of the countries you are investigating, and your job will be to show us the moves in a sport or a dance, or you could show how the country celebrates an important holiday.

Text continues on page 100.

Bodily/Kinesthetic Week

Focus on sports, dance, and recreation and prepare a how-to demonstration. Investigate sports, dance, and recreation in your country to find out what is popular. Choose one idea to demonstrate for the class.

Here are some ideas to think about:
1. Learn and demonstrate a dance of the country.
2. Show the class how to play a game that is popular in the country.
3. Show the class the dress and events of a celebration day in your country, like carnival in Brazil or the new year celebration in China.

Verbal/Linguistic Week

Focus on language and history and give a speech about two or three important events in the history of your country; use the language of the country to welcome the audience to your talk.

1. Research two or three important events or people in the history of your country. Create a picture for each event or person and prepare a speech that tells who, what, where, why, and when facts about the event or person.

2. Learn to speak in the language of your country so you can say hello to the class as you begin your speech.

➤ Figure 8.4. Research Assignments

Logical/Mathematical Week

Focus on numbers and comparisons and develop a comparison chart of various statistics from the country; show the exchange rate for money. Use the United States as your comparison and create a chart (see activity sheet 8.1) that compares these facts: sizes of the countries, populations of the countries, money and the exchange rates, highest elevations, longest rivers, years of independence (the years when the countries became independent nations).

Using manipulatives or homemade play money, take a trip to the market and show the class how much money (in U.S. dollars and in the currency of your country) it would take to buy a popular item, e.g., a jar of peanut butter would cost this much in the United States and you would have to pay this much in my country.

Musical/Rhythmic Week

Focus on music of your country and use your own musical ability or find a recording to share music from your country. Research music in your country. What are popular styles? songs? Who are the musicians? Pick a style or a song or a musician and share examples with the class.

➤ Figure 8.4. Research Assignments (*cont.*)

Visual/Spatial Week

Focus on art and architecture and work as an artist of your country and use that technique to create an original picture or sculpture or work as an architect and make drawings to show buildings and landmarks in your country.

1. Research the artists of your country and the works they create; select an artist and closely study his or her technique so you can create an original work using this style. When you share your original work, also show some works by the artist.
2. If you decide to focus on architecture in your country, select two or three structures to illustrate and label the structures to show architectural techniques (columns, arches, domes, etc.)

Interpersonal Week

Focus on exports and imports and use outline maps of the United States and your country to show exports and imports. Research the products that your country exports and imports and fill your country's map with pictures of items that are exported from your country to the United States. Fill the United States map with pictures of items that are imported into your country from the United States. Be sure to add a map key.

➤ Figure 8.4. Research Assignments (*cont.*)

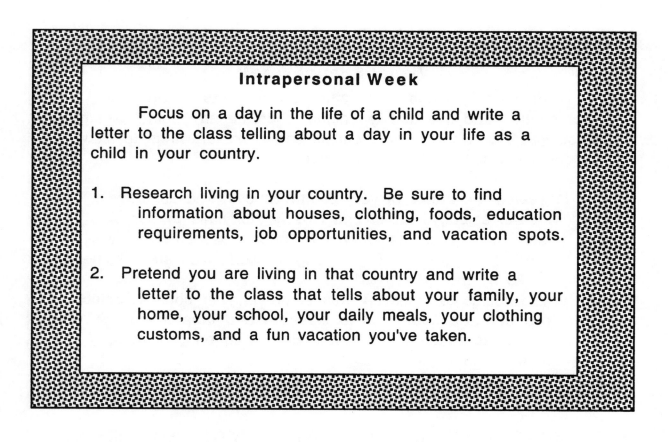

Intrapersonal Week

Focus on a day in the life of a child and write a letter to the class telling about a day in your life as a child in your country.

1. Research living in your country. Be sure to find information about houses, clothing, foods, education requirements, job opportunities, and vacation spots.

2. Pretend you are living in that country and write a letter to the class that tells about your family, your home, your school, your daily meals, your clothing customs, and a fun vacation you've taken.

➤ Figure 8.4. Research Assignments (*cont.*)

Numbers, Numbers, Numbers		
Topic	My Country _____	United States
Size (in square miles)		
Population		
Money Exchange Rate		
Highest Elevation		
Longest River		
Year of Independence		

Draw pictures of the currency of your country.

➤Activity Sheet 8.1. Statistics Comparison

In our verbal/linguistic week, we want to try speaking in several languages, at least greeting each other, and we will show important people or events in the histories of our countries.

In our logical/mathematical week, we want to compare number statistics from your country: its size, population, money exchange rate, the highest elevation, the longest river, and the year of independence. We will compare these facts to facts about the United States (see activity sheet 8.1).

For our musical/rhythmic week of study, we will share popular music of the countries.

For our visual/spatial week we will discover important artists or architecture of the countries and draw artworks or buildings.

Trading products is an important way countries and people get what they need. During interpersonal week, we will construct maps showing the products we get from your countries and the products we send.

For intrapersonal week we will pretend to be children from the countries we are investigating and will write letters telling about school and play and family life in our countries.

Connect

Move to the library and have students locate resources and begin their research, recording the information they find in their research journals.

➤ Activity Plan 3: Design a National Emblem

Materials

Drawing paper (one sheet per student)
Illustrating materials (crayons, colored pencils, markers)

Engage

Draw a symbol that most students would recognize, such as the golden arches for McDonald's, a weather symbol for sunshine or cloudy, or the degree sign indicating temperature.

Elaborate

Ask the students if they can identify what emblems represent the school districts in your area. These are usually displayed in the colors of the school district and are used on uniforms, signs, and letterheads.

Explore

Ask the students: Now that you have learned a lot about your country, how would you design an emblem that represents your country? Think of ideas that are always connected with your country and use that as the basis of your design. For example, if you investigated Australia your emblem might include a kangaroo, or you might have a pyramid for Egypt, a decorated egg for the Ukraine, or a llama for Peru. Follow these steps as you think about the design of your emblem:

1. Review your research journals to identify a symbol.

2. Think about the shape of the emblem (triangle, rectangle, diamond, circle, etc.).

3. Visualize your design, then make a rough sketch.

4. Revise your rough sketch and make a final copy.

Connect

Have students share and display their emblems, explaining why they have chosen the symbols, shapes, and colors that they have.

➤ Activity Plan 4: Culture Kits

Materials

Access to the World Wide Web (The Global SchoolNet Foundation sponsors a list-serv that posts calls for collaboration from around the world. To subscribe to the projects list, send an e-mail to majordomo@gsn.org. In the body of the message put, "Subscribe hilites." To post your own call for collaboration, obtain project criteria from majordomo@gsn.org by stating in the body of the message, "Info hilites," and to post a project description, send it to hilites@gsn.org. More information about Global SchoolNet can be found at http://www.gsn.org.)

Disposable camera

Items for culture kits (*Note:* Please refer to the "Engage" portion of this lesson for some suggested items.)

Engage

Write on the board: "What would you send?" Elaborate on the question: "What would you send if you were sending a culture kit that represented living in America?" Allow thinking time before inviting students to respond. Some responses may be items from or pictures of holidays or birthday celebrations, games,, music, school activities or information, clothing, pictures of the community, and language examples.

Elaborate

Have students decide on the contents they would place in a culture kit and create the kit. Instead of real objects, students could use a camera to take pictures of the items for the culture kits. Instead of exchanging the kits, you could send pictures and an inexpensive disposable camera (available at most drug or grocery stores) to the students who are participating. Participating countries could take pictures and return the camera to you for developing.

Explore

Create a description of the kit and post a call for collaboration to hilites@gsn.org; begin to exchange culture kits with countries around the world (see figure 8.5).

➤ Figure 8.5. Request for Collaboration

> **Request from:** (Teacher's Name)
> **E-mail address:** (Your e-mail address)
> **Institution:** (Your school's name)
> **Location:** (Address of your school)
> **Summary:** Culture kits
>
> Our class is preparing a "countries of the world project" that we will present to other classes and our families. We created a culture kit containing examples of what it's like to live in the United States and we want to exchange kits with countries from each continent. If you are interested, please let us know and we will send more information and one of our culture kits.

Connect

Display the items from the culture kits that are received and discuss their significance.

➤ Culminating Activity Plan: Sharing Days

Because this is a lengthy project, students will be eager to share products before it is all complete. The seven investigations can be combined into four sharing opportunities, and students may invite different audiences for each sharing day. Here are some suggestions:

- The bodily/kinesthetic demonstrations would be fun to present to another class; the demonstrations tend to keep the attention of the audience because of their participation potential.

- The music and speech (verbal/linguistic) products work well together and could be shared with parents or grandparents.

- The export/import maps (interpersonal), the chart of facts and making purchases in another country (logical/mathematical) could be set up as a business fair and students could invite friends to participate. Each country would have a small display of products, and guests could move from booth to booth, using play money to purchase items from the countries. In this way students could practice their exchange rate knowledge.

- The letters (intrapersonal week) and the art/architecture models (visual/spatial week) would be another opportunity for parents or grandparents. These sharing variations could be called, "May I Bring Mom and Dad Day?" or "May I Bring a Grandparent Day?" or "May We Bring Another Class Day?" or "May We Bring a Special Friend Day?" Invitations can be composed and written to follow the pattern in the book. For example:

My class and I invite you

to share in a trip or two.

Please don't be late for this day

for we'll have a lot to say!

To tell all the lore we've found

through words and sights and sound.

Please come on _____ at _____ .

9 Nine Days to Christmas

Written by Marie Hall Ets and Aurora Labastida
Illustrated by Marie Hall Ets
New York: Viking Press, 1959

Summary

➤ Five-year-old Ceci can hardly wait for Christmas vacation to begin, because this year she is old enough to celebrate her first posada (a ceremony where friends and neighbors gather and act out Mary and Joseph's journey to Bethlehem and celebrate with food, drink, and the breaking of a piñata). Preparation begins with a trip to the old market and the selection of a special piñata, then lots of baking and decorating, and finally, the hanging of the piñata. Ceci enjoys every minute of her first posada until the star piñata is broken; disappointment turns to joy when a voice whispers to her and there in the sky above the house is the brightest star she has ever seen.

Award Year

➤ 1960

Art Information

➤ Illustrated using colored pencils on dinobase.

Curriculum Connections

➤ Mexico

➤ Activity Plan 1: Sharing the Story

Materials

Hula hoop or large circle drawn on the board (see figure 9.1)
Ball (Use a tennis ball or a small rubber ball; select something that can comfortably
   be thrown indoors.)
Masking tape
Serape (or paper version of one; serapes are wool blankets, hand-woven in colorful
   patterns, and worn like a poncho.)
Rebozo (or paper version of one; rebozos are long shawls.)
Chart paper
Caldecott Award poster
The Piñata Maker = El Piñatero, by George Ancona (New York: Harcourt, Brace, 1994).
Colored pencils
Sheet of transparency film (8½ x 11)
Small cup of sand

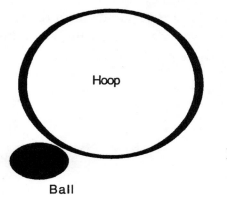

➤ Figure 9.1. Mayan Ball

Engage

Have students play Mayan Ball, a game played on ball courts in many of the ancient
Mayan cities. To play a modern version of the game, divide the class into two teams and mark a start
line on the floor with tape. Hold the hoop up or use the drawn circle on the board (see figure 9.1) and
have one student from each team try to toss the ball through it. Award one point for each successful
toss. (*Bodily/Kinesthetic Intelligence*)

Two clothing customs in Mexico include the serape and the rebozo, a blanket-like poncho
and a shawl. Display these for the students.

Celebrations in Mexico are called fiestas. Use the chart paper to create a cluster web for
the word *fiesta,* the reasons fiestas are held, and the events and traditions that happen during fiestas
(see figure 9.2).

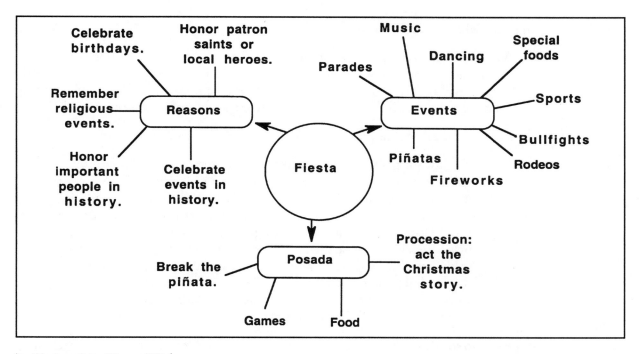

➤ Figure 9.2. Fiesta Web

Elaborate

Introduce the story. *Nine Days to Christmas* describes a holiday fiesta called the posada. Encourage students to look for details that describe how this fiesta is celebrated.

Explore

Ask the students how a posada is celebrated. (A procession starts the posada as two children carry statues of Joseph, Mary, and the donkey and lead the guests. They knock at a closed door and at first are refused entrance, but eventually are welcomed. Food, games, and breaking the piñata follow the procession.) As students share some of the traditions of the posada, add this information to the cluster map (see figure 9.2). Dramatize the events of a posada to help students understand the connection to the Christmas story. (*Bodily/Kinesthetic Intelligence*)

Connect

Return to the pages illustrating the piñata choices in the market and ask the students what piñatas they would select and why. Share some historical facts and use the pictures in the book, *Piñata Maker*, to show how they are constructed. (The custom of piñatas began in Italy and spread to Spain when the Italians traveled there. The Spanish incorporated piñatas into their religious festivals and eventually brought the custom to Mexico when Spanish explorers began their explorations.) Purchase or make a piñata for a celebration at the close of the unit. (*Visual/Spatial Intelligence*)

Share the Caldecott Award information:

1. As students examine the cover of the book, ask them what special thing they notice. (gold medal) Ask them what the name of the medal is. (Caldecott Award Medal) Ask them why it has been placed on this book. (Some responses may be that the illustrations are special, well done, particularly interesting, exciting, and/or unusual.)

2. Discuss the art techniques used in creating the pictures:

> The award information about the book describes the medium as colored pencils on dinobase. Dinobase is a process that is no longer used in illustrating. Acetate sheets (like the transparency sample) were sandblasted to roughen the surfaces, so the acetate became more absorbent (think of the sting of sand on a windy day at the beach). As you browse the illustrations once again, notice the bright splotches of colors; they really stand out against the grays and tans of the landscape and seem to reinforce the important actions of the story. The pencil lines are really noticeable in the muted colors, but much less apparent in the oranges and pinks.

3. Ask two student volunteers to search the poster for the year the story won. (Searching the poster helps students become familiar with the many different titles selected for the award.)

➤ Activity Plan 2: Mapping the Land of Mexico, Our Neighbor to the South

Materials

Enlarged floor map of Mexico (Use an opaque projector and make an enlarged map of Mexico; be sure to include neighbors to the north [United States] and the south [Guatemala and Belize].)

Five small signs (labels for the countries and bodies of water that surround Mexico; see figure 9.3)

Four arrows with directional letters (see figure 9.4)

Globe

Miscellaneous materials (yarn, tinfoil, construction paper, beads, buttons, fabric scraps, toothpicks, Popsicle sticks, etc.) for making a physical map of Mexico

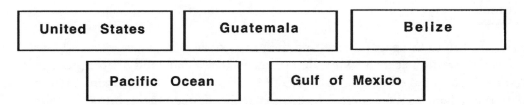

| United States | Guatemala | Belize |

| Pacific Ocean | Gulf of Mexico |

➤ Figure 9.3. Geographic Signs

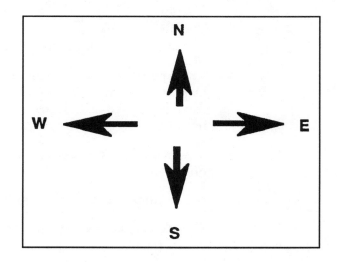

➤ Figure 9.4. Directional Signs

Engage

Gather around the floor map of Mexico and show the students the four arrows, the directional letters and the country and water signs. Identify the directions the letters signify (north, south, east, west).

Elaborate

Ask the students to name the continent Mexico is part of. (North America) Ask them: Who is its neighbor to the north? (Position the United States sign and place the "N" and one of the arrows, so it points north.) Who are the neighbors to the south? (Position the Guatemala and Belize signs and place the "S" and another of the arrows, so it points south.) Tell the students that two bodies of water also touch Mexico, the Pacific Ocean and the Gulf of Mexico. Then ask for two volunteers to use the globe to identify which body of water is located west of Mexico and which is located to the east. Place the Pacific Ocean sign, the arrow, and the "W" to the west of Mexico and place the Gulf of Mexico sign, the fourth arrow, and the "E" to the east of Mexico.

Explore

Have students work in partnerships to explore the land of Mexico, using the enlarged map and the three-dimensional supplies to create a visual image of the country. (*Bodily/Kinesthetic, Visual/Spatial, and Interpersonal Intelligences*)

Topics and instructions you could assign include the following:

1. Important waterways including rivers, lakes, seas, and oceans. Label the map and use three-dimensional supplies to create these geographical features.

2. The Yucatan Peninsula. Locate and label the peninsula; use three-dimensional supplies to show the land and vegetation.

3. The Baja, California, Peninsula. Locate and label this peninsula; use three-dimensional supplies to show the land and vegetation.

4. The vegetation of Mexico. Investigate the plants and trees of Mexico and color the map to show the vegetation of Mexico. For example, woodland and forest areas could be colored in dark green, grasslands in pale green, and desert and scrub land in yellow.

5. Mountain ranges. Locate them and use three-dimensional supplies to show them on the map.

6. Major cities. Identify the major cities of Mexico and locate them on the map.

7. The Plateau. Locate this land form and use three-dimensional supplies to show it on the map.

8. Silver and oil. Locate where these natural resources are mined and produced; use three-dimensional supplies to show the locations.

9. Animal life. Investigate the animal life of the country; use three-dimensional supplies to show models of the animal life.

10. Weather and climate. Investigate the climate of the country, create a mobile listing the weather in each season, and present the information to the class as a television weather report.

Connect

Gather around the floor map and let students present what they have learned about Mexico's land and climate.

➤ Activity Plan 3: Scenes of Mexico

Materials

Roll of mural paper
Drawing paper (one or two sheets per student for the group working on the animals of the jungle)
Colored pencils

Engage

Roll out the mural paper and explain that students will be creating a mural landscape with the colored pencil medium used by Ms. Ets in *Nine Days to Christmas*.

Elaborate

Explain murals using the following narration:

Mural paintings have a long history in Mexico. The Mayan people used this technique hundreds of years ago when they painted scenes showing rich people celebrating their lives. Diego Rivera, a modern-day muralist, began painting around the time of the revolution in Mexico (about 1910). Because so many adults in Mexico could not read, he was hired by the Ministry of Public Education and Fine Arts to create murals showing Mexican history and culture. He used simple designs and lots of bold colors. We will be imitating that style as we create our own jungle mural.

Explore

Have students design a jungle mural and create it using the colored pencils and the mural paper. Divide the students into two large groups. One group is responsible for jungle plant life and the other for jungle animal life. Decide on a scale measurement for the mural. The vegetation group should sketch and work directly on the mural paper; the animal group should use drawing paper to create their animals. These can be placed in the jungle vegetation when it is completed. (*Visual/Spatial Intelligence*)

Connect

Tour the mural when it is finished.

➤ Activity Plan 4: Ancient Cities Research

Materials

Multiple copies of figure 9.5
Notepaper (two or three sheet per student)

Engage

Write these city names on the board: Teotihuacán, Tenochtitlán, Tula, Chichén Itzá, Palenque. Review the cities and ask students to think about the city they wish to explore and investigate.

Elaborate

Review the Bloom's Taxonomy activities, and in preparation for research; help students set up their K-W-L charts, using notepaper sheets (see figure 9.6).

Ancient Cities of Mexico

Knowledge

Choose an ancient city of Mexico: Teotihuacan, Tenochtitlan, Tula, Chicen Itza, or Palenque.

Comprehension

Use the K-W-L strategy (What I Know, What I Want to Know, and What I Learned) to plan your research. List what you know about the ancient city, write questions you still have, research and write answers to the questions. As you take notes be sure to re-state your answers in your own words.

Application

Use your research to create a tourist brochure about the city.

Analysis

Meet with another student and compare your city with the ancient city he or she researched.

Synthesis

Work with two partners. Pretend you are archaeologists who have uncovered new ruins in Mexico. Design and build a model which shares the new city you've recently found.

Evaluation

Use your K-W-L chart to evaluate your work.

➤ Figure 9.5. Ancient Cities Research Directions

Note: In 1956, Benjamin Bloom (*Taxonomy of Educational Objectives.* New York: David McKay, 1956) developed a taxonomy of educational objectives as a tool for designing curricula that fosters higher order thinking skills. The taxonomy is hierarchical with each level building upon the knowledge of the previous level. There are six levels: knowledge, comprehension, application, analysis, synthesis, and evaluation. Knowledge focuses on recognizing and recalling information; knowledge activities ask students to list, record, and name. Comprehension activities ask students to explain, describe, report, discuss, and restate information in their own words. Application experiences give students opportunities to apply knowledge through demonstration and illustration. In analysis activities, students break down information into its parts by comparing debating, or questioning. In synthesis tasks, students create, compose, construct, and propose new products. Evaluation asks students to use standards or a set of criteria to assess, rate, critique, and make judgments.

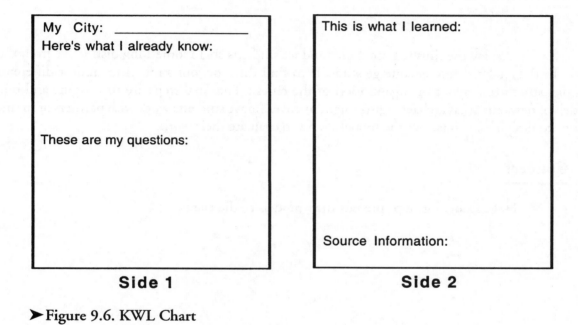

➤ Figure 9.6. KWL Chart

Explore

Have students choose research assignments and begin the process of brainstorming information they already know and questions they want to answer. To assist students in brainstorming questions have them think about information that will help make colorful tourist brochures. Ask them: If you were visiting this ancient city, how would you spend your time? (touring important buildings and places in the city, eating and resting, and attending entertainment and sporting events) Develop questions from these ideas.

Have students complete their research, then use their research notes to create tourist brochures about the cities they have chosen. Encourage them to make the brochures colorful by including lots of pictures with the information. An easy brochure format is to fold a sheet of drawing paper in half lengthwise; students can create the brochure with the fold at the top or to the left (see figure 9.7).

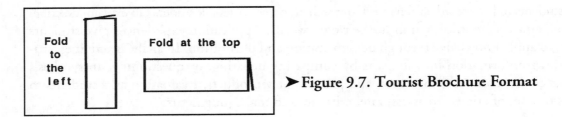

➤ Figure 9.7. Tourist Brochure Format

Display the finished brochures and let students share something distinctive from their work. In the analysis step, encourage students to find three or four similarities and/or differences (people, structures, layout or organization of the cities). The final steps are to imagine and build models of new cities that archaeologists might uncover (Have students work with partners or in small groups to design and construct the models.) and to evaluate their work.

Connect

Have student groups present their models to the class.

10 Officer Buckle and Gloria

Written by Peggy Rathmann
Illustrated by Peggy Rathmann
New York: G. P. Putnam's Sons, 1995

Summary

➤ Officer Buckle and his police dog Gloria discover what an unusual partnership they make when Officer Buckle finally accepts Gloria's unique contributions to his safety speeches. Officer Buckle knew a lot of safety tips, but he had difficulty in presenting them effectively until the day Gloria, the new police dog, participated in his presentation. Much to his surprise the children clapped and cheered after this presentation and carefully followed all the safety tips; there wasn't a single accident during the week. When Officer Buckle discovers the real reason for the attention of the children he is dismayed and disheartened and refuses to give any more speeches. He returns to his safety tip presentations only after a note from a student helps him feel valued again and think of his best safety tip of all: Always stick with your buddy.

Award Year

➤ 1996

Art Information

➤ Illustrated using watercolors and ink.

Curriculum Connections

➤ Safety, teamwork

➤ Activity Plan 1: Sharing the Story

Materials

Safety stars (One per student; see activity sheet 10.1.)
Extra copies of the book for small group use
Drawing paper (one sheet per student)
Illustrating materials (paints, crayons, markers, or colored pencils)
Caldecott Award poster
Watercolor paints (available at art stores)
Pen and ink or a narrow-point black marker

Engage

Have students gather in two circles and use teamwork to untangle the circles. Give them the following directions:

1. Stand in a circle.

2. Reach across the circle and grasp right hands with each other.

3. Reach across the circle again and grasp left hands with different partners.

4. With patience and laughter, begin the process of untangling; you may not let go of each other's hands and must step over, crawl under, bend, and squeeze through to accomplish the task. (*Note:* If students become discouraged and really don't want to continue, allow them to stop.)

5. When you are untangled we will discuss the process. What facilitated the unraveling? How did teamwork help? What is teamwork? How do you make it happen? What gets in the way? (*Bodily/Kinesthetic Intelligence*)

Elaborate

Introduce the book and encourage students to think about how Gloria and Officer Buckle would define teamwork.

Explore

Ask the students: How would Gloria and Officer Buckle define teamwork? How did the partnership between Officer Buckle and Gloria make the safety messages more effective? (Gloria's actions caught the students' attention, provided some humor, and reinforced Officer Buckle's safety messages.)

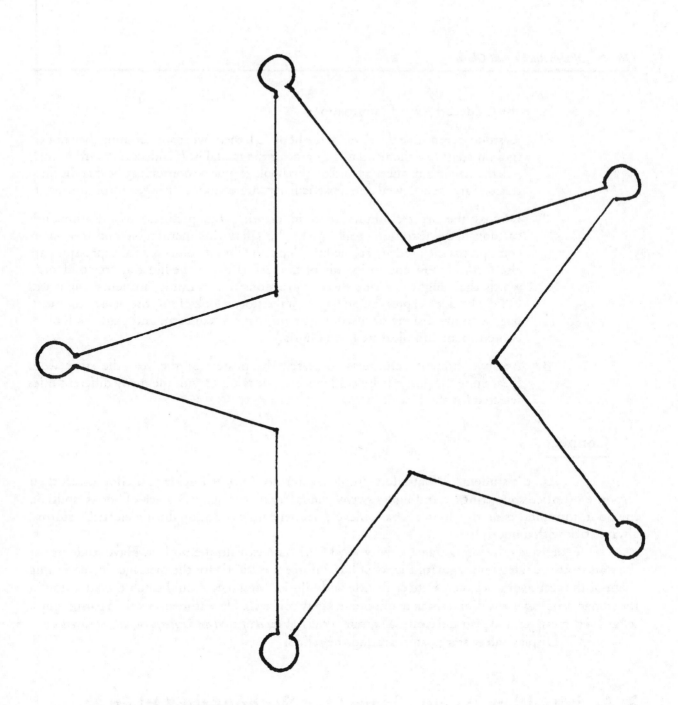

➤Activity Sheet 10.1. Safety Star

Share the Caldecott Award information:

1. As students examine the cover of the book, ask them what special thing they notice. (gold medal) Ask them what the name of the medal is. (Caldecott Award Medal) Ask them why it has been placed on this book. (Some responses may be that the illustrations are special, well done, particularly interesting, exciting, and/or unusual.)

2. Discuss the art techniques used in creating the pictures. Ms. Rathmann's cartoon-like illustrations really make the safety tips memorable and the watercolor paints she used are applied in deep and vibrant colors. Facial expressions are also fun to follow and easily mirror the text. (Browse the illustrations to identify words that might describe these expressions; for example, students might call Officer Buckle's expression on page 1 of the story a look of surprise or astonishment, page 2 shows dismay or discouragement, page 3, concern, and page 4 a look of contentment and pleasure from Gloria.)

3. Ask two student volunteers to search the poster for the year the story won. (Searching the poster helps students become familiar with the many different titles selected for the award.)

Connect

Ask the students: What safety problems concern Officer Buckle and Gloria? List their responses. (untied shoestrings, standing on swivel chairs, trying to balance a stack of books, spills on the floor, thumbtacks on the floor or chair, bicycle helmets, no swimming during electrical storms, always stick with a buddy)

Display the safety stars (activity sheet 10.1) and explain the project. Have students use the stars to create safety messages for the school. Reinforce the criteria for the messages by reminding them of the teamwork between Officer Buckle and Gloria. Messages should catch the attention of the students, be easy to read, and speak to important safety concerns. Have students work in partnerships, select safety messages, and plan and create safety star posters. (*Visual/Spatial and Interpersonal Intelligences*)

Display safety star posters around the school.

➤ Activity Plan 2: Can't Have One Without the Other

Materials

Jars of peanut butter and jelly

Engage

Tell the students: There are lots of teamwork patterns in our world where something is missing without the other. (Show the jar of peanut butter.) Ask them: What usually teams with peanut butter? (jelly; write *peanut butter* and *jelly* on the board, then point to a table.) What usually accompanies a table? (chairs; write *table* and *chairs* on the board.)

Elaborate

Ask the students: What are other examples of teamwork? (Some responses may be pen and ink, horse and carriage, water and waterbed, mortar and pestle, bat and ball, Tom and Jerry, Calvin and Hobbs, hand and glove, Winnie the Pooh and Christopher Robin, needle and thread, smoke and fire, pencil and paper, thunder and lightning, stars and stripes, meat and potatoes, bread and butter, peaches and cream.)

Explore

Have students select ideas from the list, then fold pieces of paper in half and begin to plan the illustrations that show how the partners would be lost without each other (e.g., what would Tom do without Jerry . . . chase elephants instead: students would draw a picture of Tom chasing elephants on one half of the paper; what would happen to Jerry without Tom? . . . with no exercise, he becomes so fat he can't leave his hole: students would draw a fattened version of Jerry, possibly stuck in the doorway of his hole).

Connect

Have students add color to final illustrations and gather the contributions into a class book entitled, "Can't Have One Without the Other: Lessons in Partnership." Share the book. (*Visual/ Spatial Intelligence*)

11 Ox-Cart Man

Written by Donald Hall
Illustrated by Barbara Cooney
New York: Viking Press, 1979

Summary

➤ In October, Ox-Cart Man hitched up his ox, packed his cart with all the things he and his family had made or grown during the year, and made the long trek from the New Hampshire inland hills to Portsmouth Market on the coast. He sold the wool, the shawl, and the mittens, the candles, shingles, and birch brooms, the food products (potatoes, apples, honey, turnips, cabbages, and maple sugar), the goose feathers, the ox cart, and even the ox. Then, before returning home he walked through the market buying the supplies his family would need throughout the coming year.

Award Year

➤ 1980

Art Information

➤ Painted in acrylics on gesso-coated boards.

Curriculum Connections

➤ Pioneer life

➤ Activity Plan 1: Sharing the Story

Materials

Parent volunteers or older students (to help with the math problem solving)
Pedometer (measures distances while walking or running; available at most sporting goods stores.)
One math manipulatives kit per group (Each kit should include twenty-four clock faces, one for each hour of the day, and forty to sixty math tiles.)
Math solutions chart (See activity sheet 11.1.)
Map of New Hampshire
Jar of pennies
Caldecott Award poster
Acrylic pigment (available at art stores)
Gesso (available at art stores)

Engage

As a class, pretend to be pioneers and take a long walk around the school; walk slowly and use a watch and the pedometer to time and measure the walk. Record the time and length of the walk and help students figure out how long it would take them to walk one mile. Depending on their abilities with time, figure the amount to the half hour or to the hour; for example, if students walked one-half mile in fifteen minutes, that would be one mile in thirty minutes or two miles in an hour. (*Bodily/Kinesthetic and Logical/Mathematical Intelligences*)

Elaborate

Have students work in small groups mentored by adults or older students, using the math manipulatives kits to solve this math problem: If a pioneer walked at the speed we walked around the school, how many miles could a pioneer walk in two days? Tell students that as they figure out the answer they shouldn't forget meals and sleeping time. Share and record responses from each group and begin to fill in the chart (see activity sheet 11.1).

Explore

Tell students: Ox-Cart Man was a pioneer who walked to market once a year. Let's discover more about him. (Share the story.)

Walking Like the Ox-Cart Man

Team	Sleeping Time	Eating Time	Walking Time	Miles Walked	Ox-Cart Man	Cost

► Activity Sheet 11.1. Math Solutions Chart

Connect

Ask the students: What are clues from the story that show us that Ox-Cart Man and his family lived in long-ago days? If Ox-Cart Man walked for ten days, how many miles did he walk to get to market? Help students figure out these answers and add this information to the chart for each group (see activity sheet 11.1).

Share the Caldecott Award information:

1. As students examine the cover of the book, ask them what special thing they notice. (gold medal) Ask them what the name of the medal is. (Caldecott Award Medal) Ask them why it has been placed on this book. (Some responses may be that the illustrations are special, well done, particularly interesting, exciting, and/or unusual.)

2. Discuss the art techniques used in creating the pictures, giving the students the following information:

   > Ms. Cooney prepared the canvases for the illustrations by coating them with gesso (a substance made from plaster of paris and glue); gesso coating provides a smooth surface or base for the addition of the acrylic pigments Ms. Cooney used to paint the scenes of nineteenth-century New Hampshire life. The passing seasons are wonderfully illustrated in the book; we know the story begins in fall when Ox-Cart Man loads the cart for his trip to market. (Browse the pages once again and notice the details indicating the seasons: the change in colors in the leaves, the falling leaves, the "v" of migrating birds, the bare trees and starkness of the landscape before snow falls, then the snow-covered hills, and the pale pinks and greens and whites of springtime blossoms and buds.) What details in the illustrations help us know that the story takes place in an earlier period of time? (Point out clothing styles, the wagon, the furniture and chores of the farm, the brick sidewalks, the hitching post for horses, and the general store in Portsmouth.)

3. Ask two student volunteers to search the poster for the year the story won. (Searching the poster helps students become familiar with the many different titles selected for the award.)

Locate Portsmouth on a map of New Hampshire and use clues from the story to speculate where Ox-Cart Man's farm might be located. The road Ox-Cart Man used for his trip to Portsmouth was one of the early New Hampshire turnpikes, which opened to traffic in 1803, and he would have paid 1¢ for each mile he traveled with his two-wheeled cart. Have students use pennies to figure out how much the trip to market would have cost. (Starting with the group listing the smallest number of miles for Ox-Cart Man, count the number of pennies for this trip; continue to add pennies until the cost is figured for all groups. Add these costs to the chart; see activity sheet 11.1.)

➤ Activity Plan 2: The Seasons of the Farm

Materials

Two or three down feathers (available at craft and hobby stores)

Ox-Cart Man, episode 18, *Reading Rainbow*, 1984 (available from GPN, P.O. Box 80669, Lincoln, NE; cost: about $25.00)

Clothesline and clothespins

Small slips of paper, labeled with the seasons (eight winter slips, six spring slips, six fall slips, and six summer slips)

Paint supplies (acrylics suggested)

Drawing paper (one sheet per student)

Engage

Blow the feathers into the air and let them float to the floor. Remind students of the closing line of the story, "and geese squawked in the barnyard, dropping feathers as soft as clouds." Tell students: What a wonderful image and how useful a bag of goose feathers might be! Ask them how a pioneer family might use the feathers. (pillows, comforters, coats, mattresses, quill pens)

Elaborate

Tell the students: We learned a lot about pioneer farm life from sharing the book, let's take a trip to Old Sturbridge Village and see another view. (Show the *Reading Rainbow* episode, which features the story. In the tape LeVar Burton visits Old Sturbridge Village, Massachusetts, and experiences life in the 1800s as he visits with an ox trainer, a blacksmith, a trader, and a printer.)

Explore

Hang the clothesline in the classroom or hallway and place the seasonal slips in a basket. Have students draw assignments from the basket and use acrylic paints to create detailed, colorful pictures illustrating the seasonal events from the book. For example, a student who chooses a spring slip of paper may wish to paint a scene showing the family planting the garden; a student who selects winter might paint Ox-Cart Man splitting shingles; a student choosing summer must let his or her imagination run free and create a scene in summer at Ox-Cart Man's farm. Have the students label the drawings by seasons and add descriptive sentences.

Connect

After students present their paintings, use clothespins to hang completed drawings on a clothesline in the sequence of the seasons. (*Visual/Spatial Intelligence*)

➤ Activity Plan 3: Then and Now

Materials

Clock with a second hand
Tablet paper (one sheet per student)

Engage

Have students use their hands to clap a variety of patterns. Ask them to estimate the amount of time it takes to clap each pattern. Repeat a pattern and predict the amount of time that has passed; test the prediction using the clock with a second hand. Ask students: Was it easy to tell an accurate time? If a pioneer family didn't have a clock, how would they tell time? (shadows, the sun's place in the sky, candles, sundials, hour-glass timers)

Elaborate

Walk outside and explore shadows as a way of telling time. Ask the students: Where is the sun? How does the position of the sun tell us the time of day? What kinds of shadows are created at various times of the day? What are the challenges in using the sun as a time clock? (What if it's a cloudy day? Can it really be specific?)

Explore

Have students work with partners to contrast their lives with the life of Ox-Cart Man and his family. Have them make "Then and Now Charts" (fold tablet paper in half the long way) and think about these areas: transportation, exercise, recreation, clothing, food, hardships, luxuries, jobs/chores, education. If students are stumped for ideas, use figure 11.1. (*Logical/Mathematical and Interpersonal Intelligences*)

Connect

Have students share one or two ideas from their charts, then display the charts.

Comparing Our Lives	
Then	**Now**
Traveled in a wagon or cart, on horses, or by walking	**Travel in automobiles, trains, and jets.**
Worked on the farm to get physical exercise.	**Go to a health club, participate in sports, lift weights.**
Walked to market once or twice a year.	**Go to stores anytime I want.**
Made candles and used them for light.	**Use electricity for light.**
Cooked over an open fire in a pot.	**Cook in microwaves and ovens.**
Made yarn, wove cloth, sewed clothes.	**Buy clothes or cloth at the store.**
Played tag, whittled, embroidered.	**Play video games.**

➤ Figure 11.1. Then and Now Comparison Chart

➤ Activity Plan 4: Experiencing the Life of a Pioneer

Materials

Parent volunteers (at least four)
Activity sheet 11.2, Herb Research Sheet (one per student)
Fresh herb sprigs (available from grocery stores, a local gardener or nursery, or the garden society)
Embroidery thread and needles (available at cloth stores and craft and hobby stores; remind students of safety rules for using needles.)
Two or three small embroidery hoops (available at cloth stores and craft and hobby stores)

Muslin squares printed with letters of the alphabet (available at cloth stores; use commercially prepared, iron-on letters or masking tape to secure the edges of the squares to the table, and lightly sketch the letter with a pencil. See figure 11.2.)

Fabric crayons or markers (available at most craft and hobby stores)

Masking tape

Ring Taw circle and taw line (Use an open space in the classroom or the hall and draw a circle and a taw line in preparation for the game. See figure 11.3.)

Marbles

Apple "bee" supplies: apples (one per student plus one or two extra); apple corer, knives (students can use regular dinner knives, not sharp knives); and twenty-four-inch lengths of string (one piece per student)

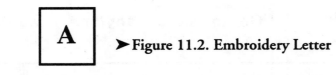

➤ **Figure 11.2. Embroidery Letter**

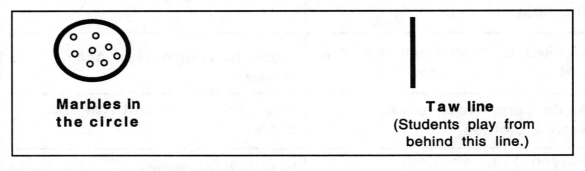

Marbles in the circle

Taw line
(Students play from behind this line.)

➤ **Figure 11.3. Ring Taw**

Engage

Slice one of the apples into thin slivers and distribute the slivers to each student. As they are eating the apple pieces, pose this question: How would Ox-Cart Man and his family preserve the barrel of apples for their winter meals? (store them in a cool place, dry or can them, make applesauce or cider)

Elaborate

Introduce the four discovery centers and explain the directions for each center.

Herb	
Describe its smell.	Select an herb sprig and tape it in this space.
Describe its taste.	
What are its cooking uses?	
What are its medicinal uses?	
What are its household uses?	
Fact sheet prepared by:	

➤Activity Sheet 11.2. Herb Research Sheet

HERB TASTING

Herbs were an important part of pioneer lives; bundles of parsley, sage, marjoram, rosemary, and marigolds often hung from the rafters and were used in cooking and for medicines. We have a selection of fresh herbs for you to taste; when you work in this center it will be your job to select an herb and use the herb research sheet (see activity sheet 11.2) to discover its flavors and uses. (*Verbal/Linguistic and Bodily/Kinesthetic Intelligences*)

THE SAMPLER

In his journey to market, Ox-Cart Man purchased an embroidery needle for the family sewing. Embroidered samplers were found in many pioneer homes; they usually had on them pictures of flowers and houses and the alphabet or religious verses. In this center you will have an opportunity to use the backstitch to embroider a letter, and when the stitching is complete, you can use fabric crayons or markers to add decorative details such as flowers, animals, or houses. We will mount the finished letter samplers in construction paper frames and display them with the seasons timeline. (*Bodily/Kinesthetic Intelligence*)

(*Note:* Even though only the daughter received the embroidery needle in the story, this is an activity for both boys and girls. Keep thread lengths short for more manageability and encourage students to work slowly and carefully. When the stitching is completed, remove the muslin square from the embroidery hoop and use masking tape to secure the edges firmly so students can add pictures with markers or fabric crayons. Use construction paper sheets to frame each sampler.)

RING TAW

Ring Taw was a marble game played by early American pioneer children. To play the game, we have drawn a circle on the ground and filled it with marbles; we have also drawn a line called a "taw" at a distance from the ring When it is your turn to play, you choose a marble that will be your "shooter," shoot from the "taw," and try to knock marbles out of the circle. The person with the most marbles wins the game. (*Bodily/Kinesthetic Intelligence*)

Directions:

1. Each player select a "shooter" marble; place the remaining marbles in the circle.

2. To determine who goes first, each player will bowl a marble from the taw toward the circle, and the person who comes closest to the circle without going into the circle goes first.

3. Continue playing clockwise from this person.

4. Each player will shoot a marble from the taw into the ring. If you knock out a marble, you keep it and continue shooting until you miss. If a taw (shooter) marble stays in the ring after being shot, you must replace all of the marbles you have knocked out of the ring.

5. Play continues until all the marbles are knocked out of the ring.

APPLES, APPLES, APPLES

Drying foods was a way for pioneers to have fruits and vegetables during the long winter months, and apple "bees" were often held after the fruit was picked in the fall. Everyone participated in peeling, coring, and slicing the apples. For drying the apple slices were placed in huge nets hung between trees or they were hung on strings in warm, airy spaces. We will participate in our own apple bee. In the center you will each have an apple to slice and string and hang for drying. Don't forget to wash your hands before coming to this center. Keep the slices thin, about one-half inch. String the slices and hang them in warm, dry places. In about a week, the apples should be dry and ready to be stored in a glass jar. (*Bodily/Kinesthetic Intelligence*)

(*Note:* As student groups come to the center, remind them again about washing their hands; while they are completing that preparation, core the apples they will be slicing. Show the students how to slice the apples.)

Explore

Divide the class into four teams and have them move to the centers. Circulate as students work to judge how much time is needed before students shift to the second center. Continue this process until students have experienced all the centers.

Connect

Ask the students: From your experiences during the pioneer unit, what statements would you make about the life of a pioneer? Some responses may be:

1. Pioneer families grew and made almost everything they used.

2. Pioneer families did not go to market or the general store very often.

3. Everyone in the family had chores.

4. Pioneer families had everyday chores and they also participated in seasonal activities like tapping the maple trees for syrup, shearing the sheep, and planting and harvesting the crops.

12 Where the Wild Things Are

Written by Maurice Sendak

Illustrated by Maurice Sendak

New York: Harper & Row, 1963

Summary

➤ Max makes mischief of one kind or another and is sent to bed without any supper, where suddenly he escapes to the land of the wild things. In this land he can be as wild as he wants; it's great until Max becomes lonely and wants to be where "someone loves him best of all." He returns to his room, where his supper is waiting and "it's still hot."

Award Year

➤ 1964

Art Information

➤ Illustrated using India ink line over full-color tempera.

Curriculum Connections

➤ Communication, with emphasis on the contributions of individuals like Alexander Graham Bell and Samuel Morse and on important developments in the history of communication

➤ Activity Plan 1: Sharing the Story

Materials

Various symbols printed on individual signs (Most dictionaries and encyclopedias have examples; look up the word "symbols.")

Music selections (to play during the dance of the wild things and to use as an introduction in the communication lessons)

Caldecott Award poster

India ink (available at art stores)

Pen for applying the ink (available at art stores)

Tempera paints (available at art stores)

Engage

Show a variety of symbols and ask students to decipher the messages they send. Have students brainstorm other examples and discuss the importance of symbols. Ask them: Why are they needed? How are they helpful? (*Visual/Spatial Intelligence*)

People can also use their bodies to communicate. Demonstrate some examples and invite students to participate in the demonstrations. Some examples are thumbs up/down, folded arms, smiles, skepticism, joy and excitement, anger, surprise, fright. (*Bodily/Kinesthetic Intelligence*)

Elaborate

Tell students: Max is particularly accomplished in sending messages with his body. Let's find out how he communicates. (Share the story.)

Explore

Ask students how Max used his body to communicate. (Making mischief, controlling the wild things, and expressing loneliness and happiness.) Reenact the story and have students focus on using their bodies to convey making mischief, showing control, and the feelings of loneliness and happiness. (*Bodily/Kinesthetic Intelligence*)

Connect

Share the Caldecott Award information:

1. As students examine the cover of the book, ask them what special thing they notice. (gold medal) Ask them what the name of the medal is. (Caldecott Award Medal) Ask them why it has been placed on this book. (Some responses may be that the illustrations are special, well done, particularly interesting, exciting, and/or unusual.)

2. Discuss the art techniques used in creating the pictures using the following narration:

> The size and placement of the illustrations mirror Max's place in the developing story line. Notice the large white border that surrounds the first two illustrations of Max as a small, mischievous boy. After he is sent to his room the white borders lessen and the pictures grow into double-page illustrations as Max takes greater control of his situation and lets his imagination grow and grow like the forest that surrounds him.

> India ink and pen created the lines that you see. (Browse the pages to examine its use.) Notice the wall coverings, the rug and furniture in Max's room, the leaves of the trees of the forest, and the wild things. (Open the India ink and demonstrate thin lines, thick lines, and cross-hatching lines.)

> Tempera paints create the colors in the illustrations. Much of the color seems muted and soft.

3. Ask two student volunteers to search the poster for the year the story won. (Searching the poster helps students become familiar with the many different titles selected for the award.)

➤ Activity Plan 2: What Is Communication?

Materials

Various communication tools (musical instrument, newspaper, radio or television, telephone, computer, magazine, paper and ink, map)

Engage

Play music, then read from a newspaper or magazine article. Tell students: Music and newspapers or magazines are some ways people communicate. Ask them: Why do we need to communicate? (*Musical/Rhythmic and Verbal/Linguistic Intelligences*)

Elaborate

Ask students: What happens when we communicate? (This is a thinking question for students while you write a message and have a student deliver it, receive a response, and return to the classroom. Make arrangements with someone close by so this can happen quickly.) Respond to the answer the student brings back with further questions.

Ask students what happened. Have them list the steps in the communication process and create a flow chart as they tell you what happened: you wrote a message, found a way to deliver the message, chose someone to receive the message, received an answer, didn't understand the answer, and repeated the process (see figure 12.1). (*Bodily/Kinesthetic and Logical/Mathematical Intelligences*)

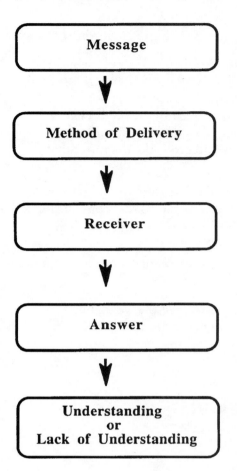

➤ Figure 12.1. The Communication Process

Explore

Divide students into eight groups and have them explore the process of communicating to reinforce and build their understanding of it. Use these communication media or select your own: musical instrument, newspaper, radio or television, telephone, computer, magazine, paper and ink, map. Each group should work with the communication medium they have chosen, then create their own flow chart telling the process of communication. Share and display the flow charts. (*Logical/ Mathematical Intelligence*)

Connect

Identify the five components needed for communication (no matter what the tool): sender, method (or way of communicating), receiver, answer, interference (anything that gets in the way of understanding).

➤Activity Plan 3: A Book of Signals

Materials

Whistle
Activity sheet 12.1, Border Page (one per student partnership plus extras for the
   cover and title pages)

Engage

Sound a whistle and ask students to identify messages the whistle sounds send (attention,
stop play in a game, start play, danger).

Elaborate

Create a two-column chart on the board, labeled sight and sound (see figure 12.2). Ask
students to identify unspoken or unwritten signals that would fit into either of these categories. Refocus
question: What sound signals are familiar to you? (horns, bells, whistles, alarms, sirens) What signals
could be listed in the sight column? (lights, picture signs, flares, flags, arm and hand signals)

Sight	Sound

➤Figure 12.2. Sight and Sound Chart

Explore

Have student partnerships choose topics for exploration (see figure 12.3) and prepare
pages for the class book on signaling without spoken or written words.
   Brainstorm the steps students should follow to successfully complete the assignment:

   1. Brainstorm or research all the signals involved in the topic.

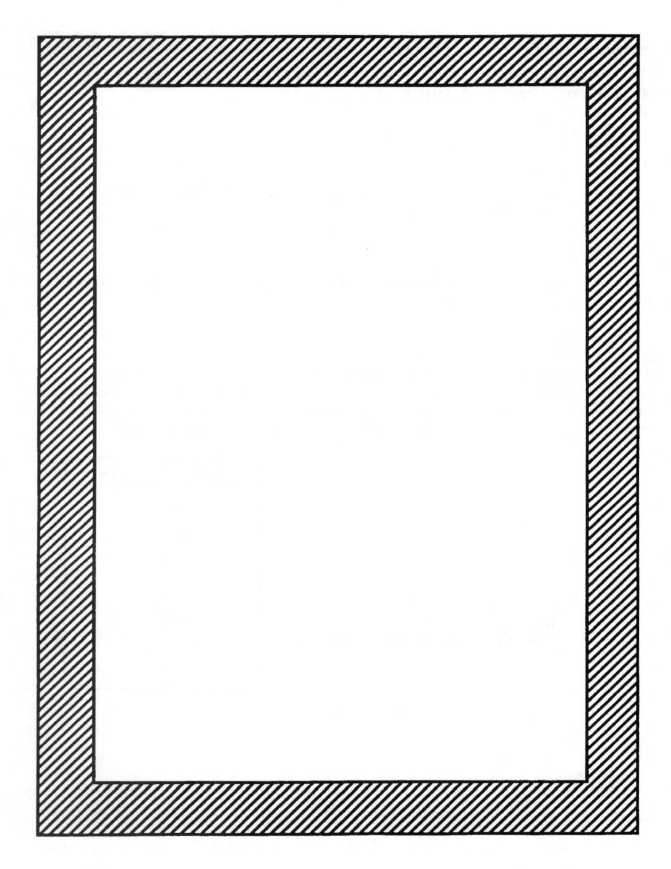

➤Activity Sheet 12.1. Border Page

```
┌─────────────────────────────────┐
│          Signals:               │
│   Topics for Exploration        │
├─────────────────────────────────┤
│  Automobile                     │
│  Emergency vehicles             │
│  Baseball                       │
│  Football                       │
│  Soccer                         │
│  Basketball                     │
│  Street/Traffic                 │
│  Flags                          │
│  School                         │
│  House                          │
│  Airport worker                 │
│  Music conductor                │
│  Danger                         │
│  Sign language                  │
└─────────────────────────────────┘
```

➤ Figure 12.3. Signals

2. Plan the illustration: How will you show the signals in picture form? What captions should be added to help us understand the signals?

3. Use the border paper (activity sheet 12.1) to create a final copy of your signal page.

Have students begin working and circulate to help them be thorough and creative in their ideas. Some partnerships may finish before others; assign the book cover and title page to those who finish early. If students are stumped for ideas, make these suggestions: automobiles (headlights, reverse lights, turn signals, brake signals, horns), emergency vehicles (flashing lights, sirens, distinctive design), sports signals (interview a referee or an umpire or use the encyclopedias to research the signals of the games), street and traffic signals (street lights, railroad crossing signals, signs for fuel, lodging, and food, other international travel signs), flags (racing, ships, semaphore signaling, flags at half mast, country and state flags), school (bells, whistles, clapping, computers, fax machine), house (telephone, answering machine, doorbell, tea kettle, smoke detector, burglar alarm, alarm clock, dryer), airport worker (How does the worker help planes move around the airport?), music conductor (How does the conductor use the baton and arms and hands to give instructions to the musicians?), danger (rattle of a rattlesnake, growl, flare, smoke, lighthouse beacon, train whistle, SOS), or sign language (look at a sign language book). (*Verbal/Linguistic, Visual/Spatial, and Interpersonal Intelligences*)

Connect

Assemble the book and share it with the class.

➤Activity Plan 4: A Look at the History of Communication

Materials

Drum (borrow one from the music teacher, use a bongo drum, or turn a plastic container upside down)
Transparency of "Writing Well-Developed Paragraphs" (figure 12.4)

Desert Life

What topic sentence would you write for this paragraph?

It's cool now and the mice and rats leave their cool burrows, searching for seeds to eat. Scorpions crawl from beneath the rocks, looking for fat beetles. Coyotes prowl for fruit or a rat or a jackrabbit. Nighttime hunting is a good way to beat the heat.

Ghost Towns

What topic sentence would you write for this paragraph?

Mining failure caused some ghost towns. When gold and silver could no longer be found in the mine, miners left to find a new place to strike it rich. Some towns disappeared because of the railroad; as long as the workers were laying the rails and building the railroad, they needed stores and places to live. When the railroad was finished, they moved to a new place and the town became a ghost town. Floods and fires could also make towns disappear.

➤ **Figure 12.4. Writing Well-Developed Paragraphs**

Engage

Play the drum. Tell students: Drums were a way of communicating messages in tribal societies; a tribesman would beat a signal to another village, warning of danger, announcing a hunt, or sending an invitation for a feast. Ask them: How did people communicate before the telephone, the computer, and the radio or television? (Invite speculation to get students thinking about a variety of research possibilities.)

Elaborate

Have students select research topics (see figure 12.5) and conduct research.

➤ Figure 12.5. Research Topics

Communications History: Research Topics
Beacons
Carrier pigeons
Telegraphs
Pony Express
Telephones
Radios
Computers
Cell phones
Televisions
Digital televisions
Video cameras
Satellites
Printing presses
Tapes (cassettes)
Compact discs
Records
Microphones
Cameras
Facsimile machines
Newspapers
United States Post Office
Cables and wires

Explore

When most students have finished their research and are ready to prepare final products (a paragraph of information and an illustration or model), model writing a well-developed paragraph: topic sentence, supporting detail sentences, concluding sentence. Tell students: A topic sentence introduces the subject of the paragraph, for example, "Many insects live in my backyard or helicopters fly in unusual ways." Ask them what topic sentences would work for the paragraphs in the transparency of figure 12.4.

Tell students that supporting detail sentences explain, give examples, and elaborate on the topic sentence, for example, "Hundreds of ladybugs crawl in the wildflower plot, a monarch butterfly floats lazily from sunflower to sunflower, a neon green and black caterpillar chews tomato leaves, and ants scurry up and down the tree to their home in the ground." Ask them what supporting detail sentences they would add to the paragraph on helicopters and how they fly. Refocus question: What are flight movements of the helicopter? (hover, take off vertically, fly in any direction)

Have students create some additional supporting detail sentences for the opening line from *Where the Wild Things Are*:

> "Max made mischief of one kind or another." We have two examples from the story: Max hammered a nail into the wall and chased his dog with a fork. What other mischief might happen? (Have students work with partners, think of other examples of mischief, and compose supporting detail sentences. As students share their sentences, list the ideas on the board.)

Tell students that the concluding sentence sums up the paragraph and closes the paragraph, for example, "All of these insects make great foods for the birds or the flight movements of the helicopter make it useful for rescue and delivery missions."

Have students turn their research notes into well-developed paragraphs. Circulate to help them compose effective topic sentences, then have them work on supporting detail sentences and concluding sentences. Once paragraphs are written in final form, have students draw pictures or make models of their communication tools.

Connect

When students have completed their paragraphs and drawn pictures or created models, assemble a timeline, having the students organize their reports in order by year of invention. Then have students read their paragraphs as you tour the timeline. Present the information in chronological order, so students really see the development of communication tools and methods.

➤ Activity Plan 5: More About Communication

Materials

> Copper wiring
> Tin cans
> Camera (digital or Polaroid)
> Copies of Blank Senses Web (activity sheet 12.2)
> Completed Senses Web (figure 12.6)

Engage

Sender, medium, receiver, answer, interference: Write these words on the board and review their connections to the communication process. The sender is the person or company sending the message, the medium is the equipment used to send the message, the receiver is the audience or person who gets the message, the answer is the response or reaction to the message, and interference is anything that gets in the way (static, lack of understanding, interruption).

Elaborate

Introduce the discovery center investigations as follows:

The discovery centers will be opportunities for each of you to choose an area of interest that you would like to explore in more detail. Here are the choices: Two of the centers ask you to look at inventors in communication, Alexander Graham Bell and how he discovered the telephone, and Samuel Morse and how he developed Morse code. A third investigation is the "Can you see it?" center; in this center select something interesting to photograph, then write a poem about the scene in your photograph. In the fourth center, a company has created a new product and they want you to design the packaging for the product so it will really sell. Will it be a new cereal? New and improved roller blades? Another Beanie Baby? You decide and figure out a way to package and sell the product. The fifth investigation is a look at the future; you will begin by interviewing adults and other students to find the tools they use for communication, the second part of the assignment asks you to imagine yourself in the year 3025 to design a model of how you will communicate with your best friend. (Have students indicate first and second choices, then divide the students among the five centers, matching first or second preferences.)

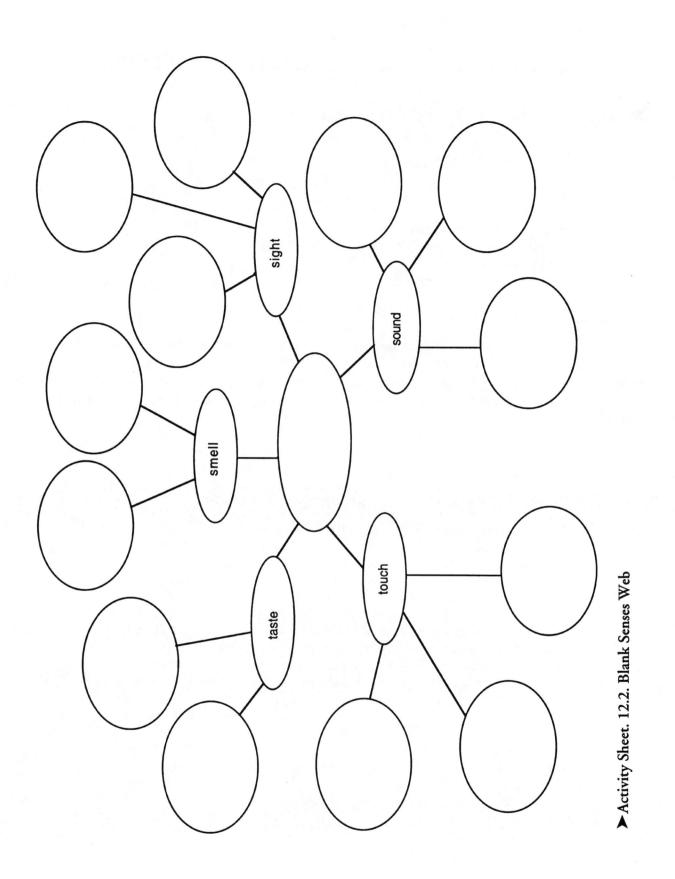

▶ Activity Sheet. 12.2. Blank Senses Web

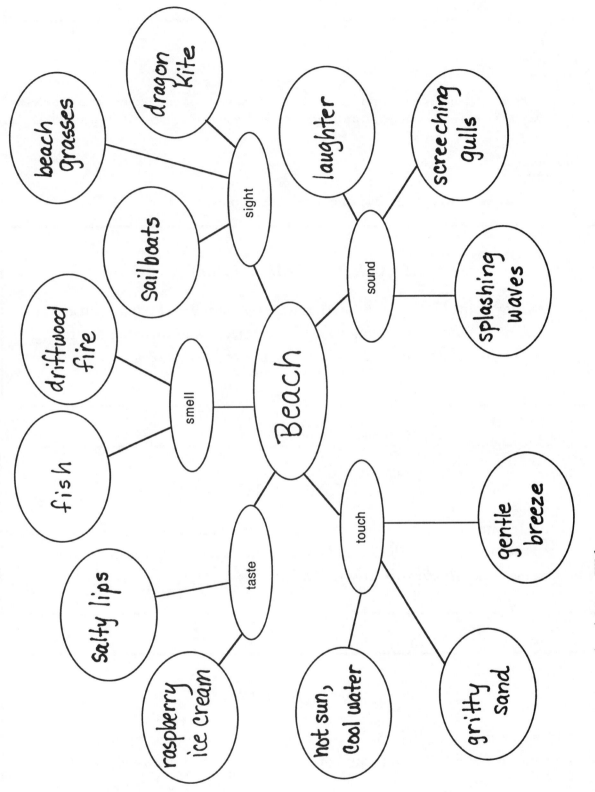

▶ Figure 12.6. Completed Senses Web

Explore

Have students begin working; circulate to troubleshoot and redirect where necessary. This will give you a sense of how students are progressing and when presentation day can be scheduled.

Connect

Have students present their discovery center products.

ALEXANDER GRAHAM BELL

Investigate the life and work of Alexander Graham Bell. Pretend you are Alexander, tell the class about your life, and create your own demonstration of his early telephone. (*Bodily/Kinesthetic Intelligence*)

SAMUEL MORSE

Investigate the life and work of Samuel Morse. Pretend you are Samuel, tell the class about your life, and create your own demonstration of the Morse code. (*Bodily/Kinesthetic Intelligence*)

CAN YOU SEE IT?

Use the digital or Polaroid camera to capture an interesting image or scene and write a poem about your picture. Use the senses web as your prewrite strategy. (*Visual/Spatial and Verbal/Linguistic Intelligences*)

WILL IT SELL?

Work as a designer. Your company has recently developed a new product and it is your job to design the label and packaging for the product. Here are some questions to think about: What is the product? How will you design the packaging so it is informative yet attention-getting? For example, pencils are tools we use everyday, but your company has invented a new and improved one. How can you help make it sell? Decide on your product, plan a rough draft of how the packaging will look, then design and create the actual packaging. (*Visual/Spatial Intelligence*)

INTO THE FUTURE

Interview several adults and students in the school to survey the tools they use for personal communication (telephone, answering machine, cell phone, electronic mail, fax machine). Create a graph that shares the results of your interviews.

Travel to the year 3025 and imagine communicating with your best friend. How will it happen? What device will you use: laser, satellite, hologram? How will communication change in the future? Build a model of this new device and demonstrate how it works. (*Logical/Mathematical Intelligence*)

13 Introducing the Caldecott Award: Randolph Caldecott

➤ Activity Plan: A Look at Randolph Caldecott

Materials

Selection of Caldecott Award books that show the gold medal

Audiovisual resource on Randolph Caldecott (*Randolph Caldecott: The Man Behind the Medal* is one suggestion. It's a video from Weston Woods, 12 Oakwood Ave., Norwalk, CT 06850; 800-243-5020; cost: $39.00.)

Picture books illustrated by Randolph Caldecott

Various resources giving information about Randolph Caldecott (Most encyclopedias have information, and you can use the Internet to access the Randolph Caldecott home page at http://www.ala.org/alsc/caldecott.html.)

Preplanning with the librarian (In addition to the book chosen as the Caldecott Award winner each year, honor books are also named. Gather a selection of honor books so that each student in the class will have one for independent reading; a list of honor books is available through this Internet site: http://www.ala.org/alsc/caldecott.html)

Chart paper

Drawing paper

Illustrating materials (crayons, colored pencils, markers)

Transparency of figure 13.1

Cinquain Poem Form

Name
Two describing words (adjectives)
Three action words (verbs)
Four-word phrase giving new information about the person
One- or two-word synonym for the person

> Eric Carle
> Bold, brilliant
> Imagined, wrote, illustrated
> *A Very Hungry Caterpillar*
> Author

Stair Poem Form

One- or two-word synonym for the person

Four-word phrase telling the location of the person

Three describing words

Name of the person

> Great inventor
> Experimenting in his laboratory
> Imaginative, creative genius
> Thomas Edison

➤ Figure 13.1. Directions for Writing Cinquain and Stair Poems

Engage

Display the Caldecott Award books and point to the gold medals. Ask students what criteria they would use to determine gold medal books. (Create a web listing their answers; see figure 13.2 for some anticipated responses.)

The Caldecott Award program began in 1938, and it was named in honor of Randolph Caldecott, a nineteenth-century illustrator of children's books and stories.

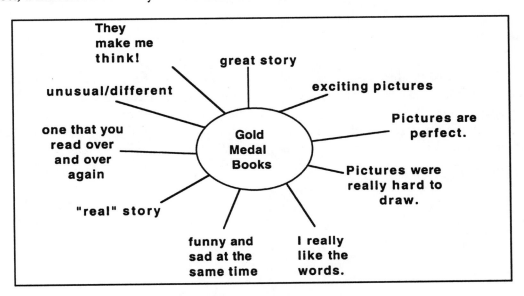

➤ **Figure 13.2. Criteria for Choosing Gold Medal Books**

Elaborate

Show the class the Caldecott program. Set a purpose for viewing: As you watch and listen, why do you think the library association named the award in honor of Mr. Caldecott? Refocus question: How was his style of illustrating "gold medal" quality? (Lifelike characters and scenes filled with humor, imagination, and action seem to be characteristics of his illustrations.)

Have students work with partners to gather more information about Caldecott. (In preparation for this research, bookmark the Internet site cited in the materials list; encourage some partnerships to begin with the encyclopedias while other partnerships use the Internet site. Circulate and flip-flop sources when you see students may need second sources.)

Explore

Use figure 13.1 to model and give directions on writing cinquain or stair poems. Have students use their research information to write cinquain or stair poems about the life and work of Randolph Caldecott. Post a portrait of Caldecott (available from the Web site listed above) in the center of the bulletin board; have students present their poems to the class. Then display the poems around the portrait. (*Verbal/Linguistic and Interpersonal Intelligences*)

Connect

Travel to the library to select Caldecott Honor books for independent reading. After students read the books, have them draw pictures of favorite scenes from the books and label the pictures with titles and authors. Before adding the pictures to the bulletin board display, have students present their pictures to the class, give brief summaries of the stories, and explain why they think the books were chosen as award-winning or honor books. (*Verbal/Linguistic and Visual/Spatial Intelligences*)

Glossary

Acrylics: pigments that dry quickly; can be used thick or thinned with water

Charcoal: soft, burnt-wood sticks or pencils

Collage: materials and objects pasted over a surface

Colored pencils: colored graphite pencils

Gesso: white pigment mixed with whiting, water, and glue; used to size (prepare) the canvas

Glaze: layer of transparent color applied over the body color

Gouache: pigments mixed with white chalk and water which become opaque when applied

Graphite: soft carbon, used in pencils instead of lead

Gums: binding mediums

India ink: drawing ink made from gas black and adhesive

Inks: transparent dyes

Line drawings: pictures drawn using lines; usually not including tone or shading

Lithographic pencil: compound of grease, wax, and lampblack

Oils: pigments used with turpentine or linseed oil; may be opaque or transparent

Oil pastels: pigments mixed with chalk, oil, and gum and dried and formed into crayons

Pastel paper: textured paper

Pastels: pigments mixed with chalk, water, and gum and dried and formed into crayons

Pen and ink: drawings made using dip pens and a variety of inks

Pigments: powdered colors made from natural (rocks, earth, plants, fruit, insects, and shellfish) and chemical substances

Tempera: pigments emulsified with oil and egg

Wash: highly diluted and thinned application of color

Watercolors: very finely ground pigments that are combined with gum and mixed with water

Whiting: very finely ground powdered chalk

Woodcuts: designs cut into well-seasoned, dried wood

Index

About the Author

Shan Glandon works in the Jenks Public Schools as a library media specialist and teaches summer courses at Tulsa Community College. She is active in the Oklahoma Library Association and conducts workshops and presentations on implementing flexible scheduling and connecting the library to the classroom. In her spare time she loves to read, bike ride, and enjoy the arts (plays, concerts, museums, and art galleries).